TALENT WILL GET YOU NOWHERE

Short Stories and Essays by ZACH SELWYN

By Zach Selwyn

Printed in the United States of America
First Dirt City Press paperback edition, 2013

ISBN: 0983723737

ISBN-13: 9780983723738

Foreword

I know you are not reading this. Nobody ever reads the 'foreword' of a book. But, in case you are, I just wanted to point out a few things before you dive into these silly little stories. First of all, I am not some pseudo-celebrity who thinks he can sell the world a vegan cookbook featuring my homemade 'Quinoacamole' or recipe for 'Soysters.' No. I'll leave that to the Bethany Frankels (whoever that is) and Octomoms of the world. (By the way, have you read Sheryl Crow's Rock-n-Roll flavored cookbook called "If It Makes You Healthy (It Can't be that Bad)?" I wouldn't recommend it.)

I also think I am safe in assuming that this publication will not lead to a worldwide book tour, Hemingway-like visits to Spanish bullfights and a deli sandwich named after me at the Carnegie. (For the record, it would feature turkey pastrami, sow's ear, cole slaw, hot mustard, turmeric, cornichons, tomatoes, Havarti dill, Russian dressing and a pluot). No, this is simply a fun project that the glorious internet has allowed me to do. If you laugh, I'm happy. If you think I'm a decent writer, I'm even happier. If you think I suck, I understand. After all, my writing credits are a now defunct marijuana magazine and a bunch of college humor newspapers that mainly served their purpose as blankets for homeless people in the 90's. Plus, a gaggle of TV shows and web series that you haven't seen. I did spend years of my life trying to get published and respected as a writer and it truly was a dreaded time… Now I am finally just having fun and enjoying the process of writing stories again. I hope you have a little fun too.

Now if you excuse me, I have to go to mash up some vegetables to make some Yamburgers.

Bio

ZACH SELWYN woke up one day in his mid-thirties and wondered where his youth had gone. He used to be an avid concert-goer, a late night party hound, a decent basketball player, a lead singer of an outlaw country-rock band, a camper, a sports nut, a musical comedian, a writer, a free spirit, and an adventurer. Suddenly, he found himself scrabbling for some sort of redemption while hosting cable television shows, raising two young children, and typically going to bed at 9:00 at night.

After digging up back issues of *28th Street*, the cult magazine that he wrote humorous short stories for in college, he recognized that he still had quite a bit to say. These essays follow our hero as he attempts to reclaim his lost youth while still being a responsible parent. In Selwyn's journey through guilt-ridden hangovers, embarrassing moments and a keen awareness that his onetime charm might be fading fast, it's his funny and honest storytelling that shines in the book. Originally published on his online blog, these stories garnered him a following that demanded he publish his stories in a collection. What follows are stories that any man or woman – parent, college kid, or aging party animal - can relate to.

Zach Selwyn is an actor, TV host & musician who is currently starring on America's Secret Slang on History Channel & Guinness World Records: Unleashed on TruTV. His band Zachariah & the Lobos Riders recently released their 5th album. He lives in Los Angeles with his wife and two children.

WWW.ZACHSELWYN.COM

Talent Will Get You Nowhere

I got a phone call from my agent yesterday asking me if I'd be willing to audition as the host of a new television show called *America's Firmest Tits*.

After laughing at the absurd title and awaiting an apology for his obligatory agent humor, I was put on hold while be answered another (undoubtedly more important) phone call. After a minute or two, he returned with a time and address for the audition and asked me if I was available to make it.

I suddenly realized that he wasn't kidding.

Apparently Playboy TV was trying to launch a reality/humor block where sex and laughter came together for a, excuse me, *titillating* hour and a half. The flagship show was going to be sort of a *Daily Show* for sex that would be co-hosted by a yet-to-be-named porn legend and a somewhat famous comedian. Apparently, the porn stars they were considering were Wesley Pipes, John E. Depth and someone simply known as "Manaconda." As far as the comedians, I think it was down to Jim Norton, Ralphie May and Doug Stanhope. Apparently, I was on the short list too, but the producers preferred me for the travel show they were developing. Yes, *America's Firmest Tits*.

When I started out in show business, I declared that I would never compromise my career for money. Like most starry-eyed actors who arrive in Hollywood with a demo reel consisting of a hometown "Hoagie Hut" commercial and a VHS tape of their performance as the Scarecrow in the community theater's presentation of *The Wizard of Oz*, I was convinced I would become the next Johnny Depp within six months of hitting the Hollywood pavement. I vowed I would never insult my resume with cheesy CGI action films, sitcoms, or (gasp!) reality or game shows. After all, those were for the Bob Saget's and Alex Trebek's of the world. In my mind, I was Sean Penn.

Flashback to 1997. I was 22, just out of college at USC where enough friends majoring in film had cast me in their student movies to make me believe that I had a huge advantage over the other fresh faces in town. I sent out some really expensive headshots, bullshitted a resume, and prepared to settle into my new life as the next Redford, Eastwood, or even Cage. I got a decent manager and an even better agent; soon I began scoping the Hollywood Hills for the swank bachelor pad I would be spending my fortune on.

And then I went on my first audition.

The casting was to play some bisexual, blood-crazy demon on an episode of *Buffy the Vampire Slayer.* I was pretty convinced that I would walk in the casting director's office, nail the role of "Valterra" or whatever, and get my own spin-off series within three weeks. Didn't quite happen; in fact, I didn't even get a callback. After drinking myself to sleep that night, I vowed to never be disappointed by my failures again. I developed a thick, scaly skin overnight. I also began what would become a long pattern of inebriation, attending auditions massively hungover and wasting opportunities.

Los Angeles is a brutally tempting place for a young man. The city is crawling with scintillating women, glowing barrooms, and sunny days perfect for nursing throbbing headaches. Marijuana is everywhere. So is temptation. Drugs. Backstage passes. Fame. Tiny dresses. Brilliant dining. Cinematic history. Plastic surgery. Easy money. Wasted talent. Success and failure.

I was thrown naked into the wolves' den, equipped with nothing but belief in my talent, an ability to write stories and songs, and an aptitude for charming young women fresh off the bus from their small towns and onto my futon.

If my agent called me and told me to prepare for a *Two Guys, a Girl and a Pizza Place* audition in the morning, I would get excited…until my friend invited me to a champagne pool party with the entire Tropicana Suntan Oil Bikini Team.

As a red-blooded male, I always chose the bikini girls.

Once, when I was offered an audition for *Frasier,* I stayed out drinking until 3:30 the night before trying to convince a strip club waitress that I was the producer of *Dark Angel.*

When I got a call to audition for *Ten Things I Hate About You,* I blew off preparing for it because my buddy got us on the guest list for a *Sugar Ray* CD release party. (I still regret that one.)

Basically, throughout my twenties, I screwed up nearly every acting opportunity that was handed to me.

This pattern went on for years. Occasionally, I would get lucky and land a role on a TV show or a commercial. That led me to believe that I could party and s*till* book jobs. After all, I had heard that Jack Nicholson was high in 90 percent of his roles. Sean Penn? Robert Downey, Jr.? Fall down drunks, right? Shit, even Ewan McGregor had mentioned that he occasionally drank on set to get through some rough scenes. I decided that functional drinking was a totally sustainable way to follow my dreams. No wonder I never got cast on any of those shows.

That might also explain why now, at 37-years-old, I am being offered auditions for shows called *America's Firmest Tits.*

After my dalliance with drinking passed and I found myself still DJ-ing Bar Mitzvahs at 28, I got a break as a contestant on an ESPN show called *Dream Job.* I didn't win the *SportsCenter* anchor spot, but it changed my life and my career, and I was supremely lucky to have moved up at all in this town. After all, most of my old friends from my twenties are long gone from Hollywood, having packed it in after too much rejection and settling into their lives as real estate salesmen in places like Scottsdale. I was the lucky one; I squandered audition after audition but was still given a chance to be on television. Since that small break I have been the host of a dozen or so shows, and I consider myself dumb-lucky to still be in this town making a living.

Of course, no matter what success you have in show business, it is almost inevitably followed by a lull. A drought. A dry patch. And that is exactly where I found myself when my agent called with the audition for *America's Firmest Tits.*

Or, as the network preferred me to call it, *A.F.T.*

"I didn't even know *Playboy* still had a TV station," I said to my agent when I called him back.

"Oh yeah," he said. "They're trying to re-brand and become more like TLC with reality shows and cool man-based programming."

"Are you serious?" I inquired. "How did they get my name?"

"I pitched you. Look, chances are, if you get the show, nobody's going to see it… you said you needed money, right? Here's your chance."

"I don't know, man…"

"Alright," he said. "I'm not supposed to tell you this, but you are their number one choice right now. Apparently the executive producer loved you when you hosted *Punkin Chunkin* a few years back…this is a big opportunity. And they are willing to pay…BIG."

"Send me the material."

I hung up and got the email with the audition information a few minutes later. As I opened up the attachment, I initially thought I was being set up for some terrible hidden camera show. I printed out the paragraph they wanted me to read and recited the script out loud to the empty walls of my home; they had served as my best audience for the better part of the past six years. I began:

"Welcome to *America's Firmest Tits.* I'm Zach Selwyn. Throughout the next six weeks, we will scour the country to find, locate and get our hands on the greatest and firmest set of female breasts we can find. From supple scoops to hearty handfuls, we will let our palms do the patting and our fingers do the fondling. Join me as I reach out and explore America's *true* Rocky Mountains and *real life* Appalachian peaks – and find what we determine to be … America's firmest tits."

I am not making this up.

After reciting that brilliant opening monologue, they explained that I would actually be auditioning with a female model on camera, who would act as a small town girl from America's heartland, hoping to break into the lucrative breast modeling industry. I would ask a few questions about her background, inquire why she decided to enter the contest, and then *properly feel her up,* explaining to the audience exactly what her boobs felt like.

They requested that I be as descriptive as possible, including such notable details as texture, evenness, and buoyancy… Buoyancy?

When I was 22 and doing everything I could to crash Playboy Mansion parties to no avail, this might have been the television gig of a lifetime. However at 37, with two kids and a wife, I suddenly felt for the first time in my television and film career that I might be at the end. I summoned my wife into my office to tell her about the show possibility and to see what she thought about me even going on the audition. After all, my agent said I was their top choice and that they were willing to pay the big bucks.

"Are you out of your fucking mind?" she blurted. "You were playing 'Lysander' in *A Midsummer Night's Dream* when I met you!"

"I know, but that was a long time ago," I said.

"What about your TV credits? And that movie you're writing… I mean, you had a record deal and a recurring role on *Greek* two years ago – you can't host a show about firm tits!"

"But Playboy TV has *money*," I pleaded. "It would be nice to pay off the credit cards and the student loans and all that shit, ya know?"

"Fuck money!" she screamed. "You won't have any money if you take this job because I'll divorce you!"

I took a deep breath.

"What do you want me to do?" I asked.

"Turn it down!" she said. "You are much more talented than *America's Best Tits.*"

'Firmest."

"Whatever! Don't be an idiot. Another show will come along soon and we'll be fine… If we *really* need money, you can go work at Trader Joe's or something."

And with that, the oven beeped and she was off to feed the children.

I thought it over. Trader Joe's versus an opportunity to travel across America feeling up 21-year-old girls for the next few months. Handling groceries, or handling perfection? I drank three glasses of red wine, called my agent, and told him I needed to sleep on it.

Every man has a few missed sexual opportunities in his life: a girl who he regrets not sleeping with at a certain time, an ex-girlfriend he could have mustered up one last fling with three years later, even advances he turned down because he was too stoned or drunk and afraid of failing to perform. When you've been married for eight years, these lost moments become more excruciating to a man because he thinks that he may have missed out on something spectacular that will never happen again. That night, as I lay in bed, I knew that turning this TV show down would be the ultimate "girl I could have made out with, but didn't".

I ran up Bronson Canyon the next morning and surveyed the smog-drenched Hollywood basin below me. Once it was a crystal clear lake, full of possibility and wonder. I thought back to 1991, when I was fifteen. I wrote an Oscar acceptance speech where I thanked a bunch of made up people from a long list; I thanked my mother for exposing me to theater and for taking me to every movie that opened, and I even thanked my imaginary wife, Meg Ryan, for sticking by me all those years. I mentioned what an honor it had been to be blessed with such a tense and dramatic role, to have a chance to explore a darker side of human emotion. At the very end of the speech, as I wiped away tears, I thanked my high school drama teacher Robert Burroughs for encouraging me to follow my dreams and go out to Hollywood…

As I looked out at the polluted dreamland below me, I thought a lot about that fake speech. I was so convinced it was going to be a reality that I had laminated the paper it was written upon and tucked it away in my journal. Now I wondered where that journal even was.

I spent a few minutes ruminating about the blown auditions of my younger years, the late nights that ultimately led nowhere, and the odd twists and turns my career had taken to bring me to this point. I felt like the chances of ever reading that Oscar acceptance speech were slowly slipping away. But then again, this is Hollywood. Nowhere else do you have a better chance of re-inventing yourself and coming back again and again. If you're willing to stick it out through the tough times and not take every crappy script that is thrown at you for financial reasons, you might just have a little longevity in your career and find yourself in a remarkably different place a few years down the line.

I thought about *America's Firmest Tits*; it didn't exactly seem like a step in the right direction. In fact, it might be the kind of show that guarantees I will never get to stand onstage at the Oscars, no matter how brilliant my future performance. I thought about my house and the fact that the heat was shut off just after December because we didn't pay our gas bill. I also thought about my kids, and how disappointed they would be if they turned on the TV and saw their father engaged in heavy petting with a bunch of Girls of the ACC.

I made it home and told my wife I was turning down the audition. Her eyes lit up and she hugged me with a love and warmth that no heater could ever recreate. I took her in my arms and looked her in the eyes.

"Look, if you want me to work at Trader Joe's for a while, I will," I said.

She stared back at me and smiled. She leaned in and kissed me again.

"Don't worry about it," she said. "Some other role will come up."

Who knows, I thought to myself… Maybe it will.

All My Wife's Famous Ex-Boyfriends

Hollywood is a notoriously tough town. About 99 percent of the people who arrive here daily to become television or movie stars end up scrambling to make ends meet, strung out on drugs or alcohol, or waiting tables at some awful Middle Eastern restaurant buried deep in the San Fernando Valley. In my fifteen years here, I have seen a fair amount of contemporaries pull into town with glossy head shots, star-struck eyes and dreams of walking the red carpet, only to return to their parents' houses as quickly as six months into their silver screen adventures. Most men or women barely scratch the surface in this town. Some might land a commercial or two, or even become a member of somebody's entourage, but the majority of these illusionary dreamers end up as footnotes to the lucky ones; easily replaceable, and rarely remembered. If they're lucky, they might meet one or two people in five years who have found success.

Yet somehow, for reasons unknown, three of my wife's ex-boyfriends happen to be incredibly famous film and TV superstars.

I am not at liberty to mention them by name, but let's just say that you have seen them on screen. You have possibly bought an *Entertainment Weekly* because they were on the cover. If you're a woman (or a man), you may have imagined one or two of them in your mind while being intimate with your boyfriend or husband. You may have fainted while meeting them at Comic Con. Two of them have even been on *lunch boxes*. I'm talking huge f-ing stars.

Now, according to my wife, before she met these three guys they were simply struggling actors, living off Top Ramen and tips from bartending or waiting tables at places like the now vanished Italian restaurant "Pane E Vino." Once she broke up with them however, their careers took off and they now all own multiple homes and squire fabulous starlets across the covers of *In Touch* and *Us*.

As my wife would say, she has the "golden vagina".

In the twelve years we have been together, I have certainly created a moderately successful television career and I am grateful and appreciative of any work I've received. Yet, as a competitive man, I am very aware that I am still miles away from the careers of the three aforementioned actors whom previously shared my wife's bed.

Which makes me think the only way my dreams of becoming a successful film and TV actor will come true is if **my wife divorces me**.

I jokingly posted this thought on Twitter a few months back and received a huge amount of responses from followers trying to figure out who these actors were. Guesses ranged from Bradley Cooper to the RZA - but I would not reveal their names to anybody. In defense of my wife, she was never a starfucker; in fact, she once turned down a sexual advance from a very drugged-out Chris Farley after he flew her and a friend on a private jet to Hawaii after a night of partying in Hollywood. (She gave me Chris' XXXL green shirt a few years back; it still hangs in my closet today).

Other Twitter followers suggested the usual Hollywood cocksmen – David Spade, Jeremy Piven, Charlie Sheen, et al. The thing is, those guys were already stars before my wife even *moved* to LA. No. Her celebrity cache was founded on the strength of her sense of humor, encouragement, and her flat-out sexual power.

When I "hung up my boner" at age 26 after meeting my wife, Wendy, I had but one celebrity conquest on my "sex resume" (not including ex-Playmates and flash-in-the-pan actresses). She was an actress named Danielle Fishel, who played "Topanga" on *Boy Meets World.* At the time she was 19 and I was 22. She also happened to have dated now-out-of-the-closet 'NSYNC star Lance Bass just before she met me, so when we hooked up one night at a celebrity-filled bar called Dublin's on Sunset Boulevard, I thought I had scored an A-List hottie. (For the record, we never had sex – just made out in the bar and then my driveway for three hours).

Bottom line? Not exactly Motley Crue kind of sexcapades. In fact, when I ran into Danielle seven years later while she was hosting a show on Style Network called *The Dish,* she had no idea who I was.

At the same time as my dalliance with Danielle, Wendy was living it up in private jets, drinking with Keith Richards at the Whiskey Bar at the Sunset

Plaza, being flown to New York by record executives (remember them?) and living an all-around fabulously privileged life for a hot woman in her late 20's. I was still traveling to Puerto Vallarta with my family over Christmas for snorkeling adventures… Advantage: Wife.

How I ended up with Wendy is another story, but the fact is, we're perfect soul mates. I could not be luckier. And nobody has told me this more emphatically than her three famous exes…

I have now met them all.

Roughly three years ago I was in an electronics store when I ran into undoubtedly the most famous of these exes. He is a star on a very popular TV show now in its ninth season or something. He is cool and handsome and built and talented and I wondered why my wife had ever decided that they weren't right for each other. I approached him as he perused a $7,500 outdoor flat screen TV and weatherproof speaker system, telling the salesman it was for his "homies to watch the Lakers game" that evening.

"Hey, bro," I said.

He raised an eyebrow and gave me the once-over – not unlike how his character surveys criminals on his show.

"Just wanted to say hi – I'm a fan… I'm Zach – I married Wendy Thompson…"

His face lit up. He waved away the salesman and high-fived me. He smiled and said, "Dude! How'd you ever pin her down?"

Relieved, I laughed it off.

"I dunno, man… we just clicked!"

"Dude, I tried so hard to make her like, my serious girlfriend and she just never went for it… you must be a STUD."

I laughed and tore off a fingernail, nervously. I should have asked him for a guest-starring role on his show right there. Instead I overstayed my welcome by hanging around watching him buy electronic equipment equal in worth to the credit card debt I had recently racked up re-piping the copper sewer tubes beneath my front lawn.

Finally, after realizing what a tool I was being, I turned around and walked away. He called after me.

"Yo, Broseph - tell Wendy I said 'hi'," he said.

"I will man," I responded giddily. "Keep on keeping on!"

As I drove home, dreaming of a career like his, and the ability to walk into an overpriced electronics store and plunk down seven G's so I could watch sports outside of my living room, I thought about how lame it had been that he had called me "Broseph". TV star or not, the dude was not as impressive as I had once thought…I mean, "Broseph"? Come on. Although I had wished he had invited me to watch that Lakers game…

***

I ran into the second of my wife's famous ex-boyfriends at the 2012 Hollywood Holiday Gifting Suite – where already-way-too-rich celebrities walk around a room at a hotel and accept free useless shit from vendors hoping to get a celebrity endorsement. Believe it or not, these places exist, and a star like, say, Bryan Cranston can walk into one of these any time he wants and be handed $50,000 worth of crap as long as he poses for a picture with the product. This gifting suite was full of everything you don't really need. Nespresso coffee makers, stainless steel facial massagers, strawberry-crystal body scrubs, electronic cigarettes with Stephen Dorff's image in the box….it was a madhouse. I happened to be there because my friend was one of the vendors and he had snuck me in on the guest list. I was allowed through the velvet rope only after a crew of twenty-something girls *IMDB*'d me and noticed that I was hosting a TV show called *Immortalized* on AMC.

After drinking some horrible peach bellinis with former NBA-player-turned-TV host John Salley, I strolled through the suite hoping to get anything worth selling on eBay. It was then that I saw Wendy's ex from the 90's, a well-known film and TV star who was wheeling around a metal cart full of free stuff behind him.

After observing his behavior for a few minutes, which basically included barking orders at his suite-host and jamming as much crap into his metal basket as he could, I came to the conclusion that he must be a world-class asshole. My wife had mentioned that he had endured years of drug and alcohol abuse, but was supposedly on the straight and narrow now; still, if there was a rehab for douchebaggery, this guy needed to be shipped there immediately.

At the conclusion of the walkthrough, my suite loot consisted of two gold-plated pens, a set of thermal pajamas and an iPad charger that powered up to nine different devices at the same time. I also got a free week in a Bahamian Hard Rock Hotel…but I was responsible for getting myself there. That will never happen. Compared to the other actors in the suite, I barely registered. Nobody had heard of the AMC show I was hosting and my request for any of the bigger items was denied.

I wasn't really that insulted by the lack of attention until I saw Tila Tequila loading up her Range Rover with about six Nespresso makers.

As I waited with a small crowd for my car, I decided to let Ex Number Two know that I had been the one who snagged Wendy Thompson; it was a small victory, but one I needed at the moment.

"Hey man," I said. "You're that guy from that film, right?" I said.

"Yeah, man…what up."

"Did you used to date Wendy Thompson?"

He paused and looked me over as his suite host loaded up his Mercedes SUV with free gifts. He took a drag off his new electronic cigarette.

"Yeah, a long time ago, why?"

"Funny, I was going through some old photo albums and saw pictures of you in them… like from '97, right?"

Ex Number Two cracked his neck and stared me down. He was menacing and steely-eyed. The rasp in his voice screamed "decade-old cocaine habit".

"Why were you going through her photo albums?" he wanted to know.

"Oh, we're married and I'm sort of the 'family scrapbooker'," I replied, immediately feeling like a total dweebazoid.

"No way!" he said. "Dude, tell her I said hi…is she seeing anybody?"

This comment obviously took me aback, considering I had just mentioned that we were *married*. I came to the quick conclusion that Ex Number Two was not exactly a very bright bulb.

"Uhh, yeah, actually we're married," I repeated.

After he peeled a twenty dollar bill off a fold and handed it to his suite host, he came back and shook my hand.

"I gotta hand it to you man, she's a keeper. Don't fuck it up like I did."

"Oh, thanks. I won't."

At that point, he stared at my meager haul from the gifting suite. It all fit in one canvas bag.

"Dude, you didn't get an espresso maker?" he inquired.

The truth was, I wasn't offered one. The PR department at Nespresso did not think I was recognizable enough to warrant a gift.

"Naah dude, we have two already – I didn't need one," I lied.

"Bro, all this stuff isn't for you! I give all this shit away to my family, my sisters, my housekeeper, my agent…You think I really want a stainless steel facial massager? Hell no - my assistant is getting that!"

I nodded. He was smarter than I thought. He had just done all his holiday shopping in one spot for the price of a photograph or two. I was now pissed that I didn't get a coffee machine.

"Nice to meet you, man," I offered before he walked to his car.

"You too, man. Tell Wendy what up for me… And good luck with that! Don't do what I did!"

And with that, he was gone – off to another gifting suite across town where he would work the Hollywood system once more.

When I got home and told Wendy this story, she proceeded to remind me of his inhuman drug intake, his dismissal from two big Hollywood films, and the fact that she once walked in on him masturbating to an Avril Lavigne music video during a family dinner party. We finally agreed that he was a total loser, and I kissed her goodnight fully knowing that I was the luckier one because I got to sleep next to her. Of course, once the lights went off, she knew exactly how to make me second-guess my afternoon's actions.

"Really?" she said. "You couldn't get *one* Nespresso maker?"

***

Ex Number Three is currently one of the biggest stars in the world. He sort of stalked Wendy when he followed her to a bar called Smalls after a Social Distortion concert in the mid-90's. His indie film was a big industry darling at the time, and it would eventually garner him worldwide recognition. That night at Smalls, he introduced her to Quentin Tarantino and some other Hollywood heavy-hitters. A few dates followed, and then a tabloid photo surfaced of him with a famous stunning blonde in a Jacuzzi. Since Wendy wasn't exactly committed to him at the time, she shrugged it off and went on her way. Within a year he was starring in a huge film, and three years later he was one of Hollywood's highest paid actors. All after dating my wife.

I ran into him at the Hotel Café on Cahuenga one night after my band had finished playing. It was a decent crowd for a Thursday; we played a lively set and the owners were all excited about the future of our band. Beer and wine flowed, and we all ended up doing shots at the bar, much smaller then than it is today. It was there that I met Ex Number Three.

Getting to him was harder than the others. He was obviously out to be seen, and had a brood of beautiful women clucking at his feet. When I finally poked through the crowd to order another beer on the band tab, he stopped me.

"Your band was good, I love outlaw country," he said.

Again, I should have handed him a CD and asked him to get a song in one of his films. Instead, I brought up Wendy.

"Dude, this is so funny!" I yelled over the crowd. "I married Wendy Thompson!"

He leaned down into my space and took out some homemade earplugs fastened from paper bar napkins.

"You have a hairy Johnson?" He responded.

Like him or not, the dude was funny.

"No, haha," I continued. "I married Wendy Thompson…"

He took a minute to register who I was talking about. They had been together for two months roughly eight years earlier, but I still expected him to react a little more intrigued.

Instead, he nodded his head and said, "Did I ever sleep with her?"

"I have no idea," I said. "But you dated awhile back…"

He replaced the earplugs in his ear and looked my way once more. He obviously had no clue who Wendy was or why I was so interested in sharing my matrimonial conquest with him.

He slugged his beer and yelled at me once more.

"If I did sleep with her, that means we're Eskimo Brothers," he said.

(For the record, according to UrbanDictionary.com, the term "Eskimo Brothers" is used to describe two men who have had sex with the same woman.)

Terrific. "Nice to meet you man," I screamed.

"Congratulations on getting married," he said before turning around to watch the next band. Disturbed, I went outside to bum an American Spirit from somebody.

That night I got home and relayed the story to Wendy, who at this point, was starting to find it strange that I was running into all of her exes around town. She said that Ex Number Three was always an egomaniac who never seemed to remember people or care about anyone but himself.

"Yeah," I agreed. "He was kind of standoffish…"

We spoke about how famous these guys had become since she had dated them, and how successful they seemed on paper and in the magazines. But my wife has always been well-aware of the fact that success does not equal happiness. As we shared some wine that night and laughed at the incident at the Hotel Café, I relayed how lucky I felt to have found her and to have started our family together and that even if I never became some huge star, I would never ask her to dump me for my own personal success.

Lying in bed that night, I asked her once again if she regretted dumping any of these exes who had turned out to become Hollywood A-Listers.

She rolled over, kissed me softly on the lips and said, "Yes."

I laughed so hard, I nearly threw up on my thermal pajamas.

"Well, I look at it this way," I said. "I'm Eskimo Brothers with some pretty huge stars…"

She laughed.

"Who am I 'Eskimo Sisters' with?" she inquired.

I thought about it for a long time.

"Well, *almost* Topanga from *Boy Meets World*," I said.

She put her arms around me and smiled as I kissed her on the forehead and turned out the light.

The Return Of The Bar Mitzvah King

I have to emcee a Bar Mitzvah next week.

No, not as a favor to a relative; this is a job I am contractually obligated to do. A job I consented to nine years ago. A job that will pay me to slow dance with a 95-year-old great-grandmother as "What a Wonderful World" echoes throughout the ballroom of the Calabasas Marriott. A job that is part of an occupation so nerve-wracking and terrifying, that I once swore I would never do again. Here's the deal…

Apparently, I did such a good job emceeing Goldie Thalberg's "Princess Fairy Tale" Bat Mitzvah back in 2003 that her father Alan had booked me to be a part of his youngest child Max's Bar Mitzvah…on September 29, 2012. According to my old boss, Mike, I took a $1,000 booking fee in 2003 and signed a contract. I have absolutely no recollection of this event whatsoever, but Mike said that if I returned the thousand bucks, I could get out of the commitment. Unfortunately, thus far in 2012 I have made a grand total of $329.00.

Looks like I'm doing the Bar Mitzvah.

My career shifted right around the time of the Goldie Thalberg party; I began working somewhat consistently for channels like ESPN, G4, and Discovery. I actually thought I was out of the game forever. I have not thought about Bar Mitzvahs at all, and haven't even been to a Bar or Bat Mitzvah since Goldie's. And I couldn't be happier; for six years, it was my only job.

See, from late 1997 to December 2003, I was a part of one of the biggest Bar/Bat Mitzvah/Wedding party planning companies in the world. We monopolized the party business in southern California, sending out charismatic emcees and hot female dancers, adequate young DJ's and aging cheese-meisters with grease-pan hairdos to turn boring parties into the greatest celebrations of a family's life. The company was called You Should Be Dancing, and at one point I was a high-ranking performer, requested by Jewish families from all corners of the expansive California landscape. I sacrificed my Saturday nights for paychecks soaring well into the low four-figure range, all while making a fool of myself in front of a bunch of smiling Jews and their awkward offspring. From candle lighting ceremonies to mother-son dances, I witnessed it all. The stories are endless and the experience was invaluable, but by 2003, the minute I saw the slightest crack in the window, I escaped – and I never once looked back. Until my old boss called me last week.

"You've gotta be kidding me!" I said to Mike, my onetime supervisor. "When did I do this kid's sister's party?"

"2003, Zach," Mike responded. "You need to call them and start working out the details, unless you just want to return the thousand bucks."

Hmm. Return the money? That thousand dollars was long gone, spent many years before I knew kindergarten would cost $25,000 per year, or that "escrow" was an actual thing and not Sheryl Crow's hip hop name.

My wife and I are currently scrambling to refinance our house with some bullshit 2009 Obama-bank Re-Fi that we have been rejected by nine times already. I owe my dentist $847 for the eight – yes EIGHT – cavities he filled for my son last month. (For the record, I have never had a cavity in my life, and my kid has brushed his teeth twice a day for five years; I am sending this quack to the board for review.) I even owe my 90-year-old grandmother five grand because she executive produced the last CD my band put out, which according to my iTunes sales has netted me -$1,388 dollars since its release in 2010.

Right now, it's looking like I am going to have to emcee Max Thalberg's Bar Mitzvah. And I am scared shitless.

Back in the day, I had a pretty impressive Bar Mitzvah routine. It was cheesy and full of feigned spontaneity, but it worked almost every night. It always started with a traditional Jewish Horah, and went into me leading a choreographed dance to "Think" by Aretha Franklin, which was then masterfully mixed into the "Y.M.C.A." and "The Time Warp". Then, I'd drop the CD for a then hip new rap dance song like "Gettin' Jiggy With It" before closing the set with a popular funny jam like "Stacy's Mom" by Fountains of Wayne. Then came the obligatory Frank Sinatra send-off to get people to their tables for their salads, before I would toss on James Taylor's *Greatest Hits* and hit the open bar for about five double bourbon and ginger ales. I'm guessing that the scene may have changed a bit since then.

"Look, Zach – I'll send you out with our hippest DJ and some glow-sticks to give away," Mike promised. "It'll come right back to you, you've always been a natural performer."

"I don't know Mike, I'm so off on the new music and everything," I said. "Is Mase still popular?"

"I doubt it. But don't worry, we have a bunch of Lil' Wayne and Kanye West and Fun and all that new stuff…you'll be fine."

I took a deep breath. Who the hell is Fun?

"How much am I making again?" I asked.

"Well, since you already took the advance, I'll pay you what all the emcees get these days: $250."

250 bucks. Not bad for a night's work, but the pressure and anxiety I used to face preparing for and executing these parties was already beginning to creep back up on me. I wasn't sure if it was worth it. I opened a bottle of red wine before stumbling upstairs to give my kids a bath. As I soaked them in the tub, I sipped the genial crimson liquid and leaned back, wondering how the hell my life had led me back here.

The first time I emceed a Bar Mitzvah I was 22. It was a Saturday night during my first summer in the real world after college, and most of my friends were out at the beach sucking down Mexican beer and talking to beautiful women, deciding between playing the Rolling Stones or Snoop Dogg on some jukebox. I was stuck in a $50 tuxedo talking to a 13-year-old girl about which song I was going to play next: "Barbie Girl" by Aqua or "MMMBop" by Hanson. That night, as the familiar words to "Hava Nagila" rebounded off the back wall of the party room at Temple Adat Elohim, I nervously took the microphone and directed the Horah dance as best I could. I had the men grasp hands and come to the middle, circle to the left, stop and clap, circle to the right; I even had to bring in a chair on which to seat little Joshy Schnozzleman as he was hoisted to the ceiling by his proud parents and a bunch of inebriated uncles. I was drenched in sweat, completely unable to grasp the concept that I had graduated USC two months earlier with a Broadcast Journalism degree – and was now officially a "Bar Mitzvah Emcee". I gave myself three months at the job, thinking in the back of my head that some great acting break would come along and take me away from Bar Mitzvah hell…

Little did I know, this would be my profession for the rest of my 20's. Mike even coined a phrase for all of the employees; we had to refer to ourselves as the "Pied Pipers of Party People". I am not kidding.

By my second year into the job, I had made some good friends. We were all actors and musicians, and we had a job that allowed us to get to auditions during the week and make a decent living on the weekends. Plus, once we figured out a way to have bartenders serve us alcohol during parties, the job eased up and became a lot more fun…which led to a bunch of incredible stories.

At a wedding in 1999, a DJ named Ronnie Jacobs had sex with a bride in a broom closet ten minutes after her first dance.

Rick Freed slept with the mother of a Bat Mitzvah girl while meeting with her to organize the slide show.

Brad Billings got paid $1,000 to show a woman his dick at a wedding.

It went on and on.

Paul Rudd's name was thrown around the You Should Be Dancing offices nearly every day. Apparently, in 1994 or so Paul had worked at the company as a DJ and emcee before getting his break in the film *Clueless*. We all aspired to be Paul Rudd, and looked at this job as a launching pad for our acting careers. (Years later when I interviewed Paul Rudd, I mentioned to him that I used to work at the same company he did; he laughed and asked me how I "got out", like I had broken out of a Civil War prison camp or something.) After his break I saw Paul on a late night talk show spinning stories from his days on the Bar Mitzvah circuit, and even those yarns were entirely inspiring to every one of us; if he could get out, we all could.

After overdrawing my bank account, I realized that there was no way out of doing the party. Thankfully, it was then that I realized that this could, in fact, be a great opportunity. After all, I had met plenty of Hollywood folks at parties over the years; maybe someone would like my dance rendition of "Greased Lightning" and offer me a walk-on role on *Two Broke Girls*? Heck, I used to DJ Bar Mitzvahs that Jonah Hill attended, back when he was the funny fat kid who ate all the dreidel-shaped sugar cookies. Maybe this party would open an unexpected door I hadn't even considered? I immediately called Mike and told him I was on the job. He gave me the Thalberg's number and I dialed it up, preparing to fill out the typical Bar Mitzvah worksheet I used to live by all those years ago.

Here goes, I thought to myself.

"Hello?" Alan Thalberg said as he picked up his phone.

I promptly hung up.

Nervous and anxious, I decided to look up my old friend Rick Freed on Facebook and see if he was still working in the business. Sure enough, he was; he had branched out and started his own company called "Freed Your Mind" and was doing quite well. I messaged him and gave him my number. He called me within two minutes.

"Zach!" he screamed. "Dude! I saw you on TV last month! You're killing it, dude! How's life?"

"Not bad, Rick, how are you?" I asked.

"Still sleeping with Bar Mitzvah moms, bro!"

I was taken aback. Was he serious? He was still in the game of Bar Mitzvah MILF hunting? He must be 44 or 45 by now…hadn't the novelty of all that worn off? He reminded me of the character "Coakley" from the film *Hall Pass*. He was never gonna grow up.

Rick updated me on some of our old friends from the business: good old Ronnie Jacobs got fired in 2005 when he hit on a girl who turned out to be 16-years-old. He thought she was 25. Turned out, she was a high school junior with an Accutane prescription. Last he heard, Ronnie was DJ-ing at the Spearmint Rhino in the Valley.

Brad Billings was a weatherman in Piggott, Arkansas. He had five kids.

And Rick was, indeed, still sleeping with Bar Mitzvah moms.

"Wow, man… that's crazy," I offered. "Listen… I have to do a Bar Mitzvah next week and I'm a little rusty… can you help me out?"

Rick greeted me with silence. He sounded beleaguered as his voice dropped to a whisper.

"Are you serious, man? I don't have any positions to hire you…"

"No, no - it's not like that, man – I made a promise to a family nine years ago that I'd do their son's party and, well, it's been nine years. I have to emcee a week from Saturday. I was hoping you could give me some tips."

Rick proceeded to break it all down for me. He was a lifesaver. His main point was that nothing had changed but the pop music. The dance moves were all the same, the candle lighting ceremonies and mother-son dances hadn't changed – and they even still played Donna Summer's "Last Dance" to close the night. The only thing I might need to do is help the dancers lead a choreographed routine to "Single Ladies" by Beyonce.

"Watch the video on YouTube and learn the moves," he said. "Kids LOVE it."

You have got to be kidding me.

After thanking Rick profusely and promising him I'd meet him for a beer in the next couple of weeks, I felt somewhat relieved that I might still be able to pull off the "Y.M.C.A." and *Grease* songs, though the idea of "Single Ladies" scared me blind. I quickly Googled the video and began yelling to my wife across the house as I witnessed Beyonce and her dance partners do things the human body was never supposed to do.

"White people aren't supposed to move like this!" I screamed.

I finally called Alan Thalberg, who it turns out had been shocked that I was still available. He promised me a fun night; he said that his kid Max was trying to get him to throw a *Playboy*-themed party. Max wanted his dad to hire actual Playmates to walk around, and to dance the Horah in a throne rather than a chair – all while wearing a monogrammed Hugh Hefner-inspired bathrobe instead of a suit.

Max was my kind of dude.

Over the next week, I organized a musical playlist and rented a tuxedo. I learned maybe four moves by Beyonce and just accepted the fact that my performance was going to suck. I asked Mike to have the DJ bring the equipment so I didn't have to lug it all around, and he told me that it was all done on laptops these days. The 350-pound equipment I used to have to carry around was long gone. Everything could be run off an amp and a MacBook Pro. I cursed the hernia I got from this job in 1998.

When Saturday came around, I avoided drinking beer and watching football during the day so that I would be on my game that night. I combed my hair, brushed up on some Travolta steps from *Grease* and left two hours early to guarantee I wouldn't be late.

When I got to the Calabasas Marriott, it was as if I had entered a time warp. The same worrisome caterers were arguing over how to plate the chicken. The uptight party planner stressed out over where the chicken fingers and pizza would be stationed during the kids' dinner. Even the photographer, who had long given up his dream of becoming the next Walter Iooss Jr., looked the same. It was a black hole into 2003; except now I had less hair and no idea what these kids were listening to anymore.

When I met the now-grown Max, he took me aside and told me how he had originally wanted a *Playboy*-themed party. Instead, his parents had forced him to have a *Hunger Games* theme.

"Totally gay," Max said, the way only a 13-year-old can. "I hated that lame movie."

"Ladies and Gentlemen…" I began, my palms sweating as the first crowd entered the room. "Welcome to Max's Hunger Games! Please choose a weapon from the guest table and proceed to your local DISTRICT, also known as your TABLE!"

These kind of moments are the exact reason I quit the business for good.

The DJ I had been assigned to work with was named Gus. He was 23 and told me he was really an actor and was only doing this job for a few months until "his career took off". I laughed and wished him luck. I made sure he knew the routine: how to transition from the Horah into the "Y.M.C.A.", etc. and he told me not to worry. In fact, he had cued up every song on his laptop to play back-to-back.

"All I have to do is press one button, and we can coast until the salads are served," he said. "It's what all the big DJ's do too, like Skrillex and David Guetta – it's all total show. They get pad two million dollars to play a pre-recorded EDM track on their laptops."

Even though I had no idea what an EDM was, I thought back to how miserable we used to have it. I used to make sure I had a WALKMAN on standby with cassettes in case of emergencies. I dealt with CDs skipping, levels dropping unexpectedly, and bad beat mixes between songs. Occasionally, music would come to a complete stop in the middle of a pulsating dance set; it was a DJ's nightmare. I used to have anxiety dreams about it the night before parties. But now, all Gus had to worry about was pressing one button, the spoiled little prick.

As Max and his friends took their seats at the "Katniss Everdeen" table, I suddenly caught the eye of a stunning brunette in a blue ball gown. She was probably 21, and her flirtatious gaze caught me off guard. What was that girl doing at a party like this? It was Saturday night! She should be out hitting the clubs or dating someone like Charlie Sheen. She was radiant and young, sexy and enticing. And she was walking towards me…

"Hey, Zach," she said coyly.

It was then that I realized. This sparkling gem of a female was none other than Goldie Thalberg.

"Remember me? Goldie?"

I took a step back. Here I was, 37 and married, staring at the perfectly shaped young woman whose Bat Mitzvah I had emceed nine years earlier.

"I go to UCLA now," she continued. "I kept up with your career! You've done some cool stuff on TV! It's so cool that you'd come back to do Max's party. Can we take a picture?"

"Uhh, sure," I said, even though she had already snapped it with her iPhone.

She turned back towards her table. I caught her looking over her shoulder a second later.

"Hey, save me a dance, will ya?"

Keep it in your pants, Selwyn…

As the evening rolled along I had no problems with the old routine, but I did notice one peculiar thing about the kids. They weren't interested in glow-sticks and flashy novelty giveaway rings anymore; all they did was TEXT. Every 13-year-old kid had an iPhone and was either tweeting, updating a Facebook status, or taking photos. At one point, a group of young girls asked to take my picture. I happily posed for them. They asked if they could "tag" me, and I said sure. For a moment, I actually felt kind of cool, like I was back relating to the youngsters again, the way I used to do all those years ago.

And then, three minutes later, I got a Facebook update. They had tagged me on their page as "the douchey emcee at Max's Bar Mitzvah".

Following my terrible rendition of "Single Ladies", where I just gave up halfway through, I found myself leading a "snowball" dance amongst the kids, where everyone changes partners. It was then that Goldie Thalberg asked me to dance. I obliged, and we awkwardly embraced in the way that hormone-ravaged 'tweens often do. As I spun her in a swing-dance pattern as a way to keep things lighthearted, I happened to catch Alan Thalberg's eye. His furious squint said it all. He gave me a signal that I quickly read as, "Get the fuck away from my daughter."

I turned to Gus and told him, "Play anything fast – NOW!"

He did. Goldie went to eat dessert and I snuck off to the bar for a double bourbon and ginger ale.

"Dude, you're not allowed to drink at parties," newbie Gus told me nervously.

Two drinks later, the party was in full swing. Max shot fake *Hunger Games* arrows at his family during the candle lighting ceremony and Goldie got sick, apparently puking up champagne in the bathroom. As the four-hour extravaganza came to a close, I was relieved when I turned to Gus and announced, "Play 'Last Dance'."

Moments later, the party came to a superbly happy end. The guests sauntered back to their cars and into the San Fernando Valley night as Gus and I went to the bar for a beer before leaving. As per tradition, Alan Thalberg came up to us with cash tips in an envelope.

"Gentlemen, terrific job tonight," he said.

"Thanks so much," I responded.

"Zach, at least three of my friends have kids Max's age and were asking if you'd be available in the next few months; I'll pass along your number if you like…"

I swallowed my beer and looked at Alan. Was he serious? Suddenly, I was back on top! The onetime king of the Bar Mitzvah had returned! I was in demand! For the first time in about nine years, I experienced that feeling of accomplishment and recognition after a live performance, that sense that I had brought happiness to the family and had been admired by the crowd…it felt good. It made me think about stepping back into the Bar Mitzvah emcee game once again. After all, you never got cash tips after you nailed a take on TV.

"Uhm, you know what, Alan… sure!" I said. "Give my number to whoever you want!"

Alan thanked us again and walked away. I watched Gus gobble an olive from the bar tray before looking up from his iPhone.

"Can I ask you a question?" Gus said.

"Sure," I responded.

"How old are you?"

"37."

"37, wow! I hope I'm not still doing parties when I'm your age!" He said. "No offense, but I'm like, with the best agent now… and I'm doing a sketch show at UCB…"

"You sound a lot like me when I was your age," I said.

Gus rambled on about how a girl from his acting class had co-starred on *Rules of Engagement* and how he hated reality TV – and then he said something that made me want to punch him in the nose.

"Did you know that Paul Rudd used to work at the company?" He blurted. "Can you believe that? He's like, a comedy legend, bro!"

I slammed what remained of my beer and patted Gus firmly on the shoulder. I sauntered back to the DJ booth to gather my car keys and jacket. As I strolled out to the parking lot, I took one look back at the cracked façade of the Calabasas Marriott, and thought, hopefully for the last time:

I am never doing one of these fucking parties again.

The Last Bachelor Party

Last week, I received an email invitation to the bachelor party for a guy at work I barely know. His name is Nick. He's 33 and marrying a nurse named Rachel. The wedding is in Woodland Hills in October and the bachelor party was being planned by his younger brother. How I made the bachelor party invite list, I have no idea; Nick and I aren't particularly close and we barely acknowledge each other on the set of the TV show we work on together. We've shared a few beers on weekends and a YouTube video or two, but to say we're close would be a stretch.

In the not-so-recent past, I would have declined the invitation on sight. I'm 37. I have two kids under six. I pass out nightly at 9:47 while watching *SportsCenter*. I pee sitting down because it's more comfortable. However, I am now looking at this bachelor party as my last chance to really do something crazy.

I immediately made an executive decision. Be it Las Vegas, Cabo San Lucas, or even a local pub crawl around Hollywood, I am GOING.

See, amongst my closest friends, my bachelor party is collectively known as the "worst bachelor party of all time". Over the course of 48 beer- and whiskey-drenched hours in Las Vegas in early fall 2004, fifteen friends from every phase of my life fought over where we should eat, argued about which strip club we should hit up, and complained about my lack of participation in the "Bachelor Scavenger Hunt" game they had put together for me.

In their defense, it wasn't their fault; it was mine. I was so infatuated with my fiancee that I refused to do anything that might be considered crossing the line. I had a chance to bite sushi off the naked body of a gorgeous Japanese woman, but opted to use chopsticks instead. I decided to turn down the hits of pure MDMA my buddy Derek brought, opting to drink Miller Lite. I even turned down my buddy Ari's offer to pay $500 for me to have a double naked lap dance from two Russian sisters in a private room where "anything goes". I was a downer the entire weekend. But in my mind I was preserving the sanctity of my upcoming marriage, and honoring the woman whose hand I would slip a ring onto.

Now, looking back at that Las Vegas weekend nearly eight years later, I can't believe how STUPID I was.

Dumb, dumb dumb, stupid dumb. What was I thinking? I guess at the time, instead of enjoying the 21-year-old stripper attempting to grind my crotch into sand during the song "Kickstart My Heart" by Motley Crue, I was thinking about the joy my fiancee and I shared when I proposed to her. When the guys all did shots of a scary-looking drink known as an "Adios Motherfucker", I passed, afraid of puking or getting too drunk and upsetting my fiancee. I was in a protected zone not unlike the one Ed Helms was in in *The Hangover*. I was basically a huge goddamned pussy.

The point of this story is to kindly offer up advice to all prospective husbands out there planning a big blow-out bachelor party. My advice? Ask your fiancee if you can POSTPONE your bachelor party until you are about eight years into your marriage. Trust me, you'll need it a lot more then than you did a month before your wedding day. If I could gather my buddies again and go BACK to Las Vegas for my bachelor party today? FORGET IT. (Those two Russian strippers? Putty in my hands. Derek's MDMA? Swallowed. And that naked sushi dinner? Let's just say I would have been balls deep in yellowtail.) I'd give one of my toes to have those opportunities again. Because as you get older, become a parent and a responsible adult, those little hedonistic moments you used to take for granted never happen anymore. Case in point: last Tuesday I literally snuck out of my house after my wife and kids went to bed to go to Yogurtland. FUCKING YOGURTLAND.

Two old college buddies, Ryan and a guy who went by the nickname Chugger, were behind my "Bachelor Scavenger Hunt". They created an elaborate list of activities I had to accomplish before the night was through. If I did 75% of them, I'd reach "Legendary Bachelor Status". 50% meant I was an "Accomplished Bachelor". At 25% I was deemed "Worthy." By the end of the night, I had completed 2% of the activities on the list. The worst score in the history of their Bachelor Party game. I was not ashamed back then. I even took pride in my refusal to play along with games like "Grab a Stranger's Tits". However, every time I think about my pathetic score, I wish for a shot at redemption.

The one game I did decide to play along with was called "Bird on a Wire". It required using your forearm as a "shelf" of sorts. A pair of large boobs rests on your arm like a falcon on a leather gauntlet prior to being hoisted into flight. You hold the pose for three seconds, and your friends check the activity off of their list. Well, following a few beers at the bar in the Palms Casino, we found a willing participant. I slid my arm beneath her heaving mammaries and held it for three seconds. My friends applauded. The sheer shame of my activity hung heavily over my head for the rest of the night. So much so that when the rest of the activities came out, I turned them all down in fear of the guilt I would carry with me forever. Jump in the Caesar's Palace fountains? Uhhm, no. Start a food fight at a buffet? Forget that. Pose with a fully-clothed girl in the "Reverse Cowgirl" position on top of a limousine? Get the fuck out of here. I had done the "Bird on a Wire" thing, and I was retiring from the game. Disappointed, Ryan and Chugger grumbled about my lack of participation throughout the rest of the night.

The stereotype of men engaging in the most primitive and testosterone-laden activities directly prior to their nuptials didn't make any sense to me at the time. I thought the women I knew, like my wife, had done it right; they chose a mellow location like a vineyard or a boutique hotel in Palm Springs and treated themselves to massages and five-star dinners. They got their nails and toes done while flipping through *Us Weekly* and gossiping about reality TV. The craziest thing they did was sip mojitos through penis straws.

My friends all wanted to gamble, drink, drug, bang, and eat. When my brother caught me texting my future wife that I missed her from a bar at 10:30 at night, he promptly took my phone and told me I was not allowed to use it the rest of the trip. I was miserable, wishing that I was in Sonoma County with my fiancee at a spa retreat. So I did what I know how to do best: I drank through it.

Don't get me wrong. Many women out-party men at their bachelorette parties. About three years ago while I was playing a gig in Lake Tahoe, six jiggly twenty-somethings streaked across the stage wearing condoms in their hair and t-shirts that read "Buy us a shot, She's tying the knot!" These partying wildebeests proceeded to do Jaegermeister shots on top of the bar, flash their shaved Britney's to everybody willing to take a peek, and make out with any college kid able to tear himself away from Beer Pong. It reminded me of the terrific term my old friend, the late comedian Greg Giraldo, coined when describing a pack of drunk bachelorettes; he called them, "a gaggle of squawking twats with'A Hard Man is Good to Find' t-shirts." Perfect.

At the end of Saturday night, my old friend Rick threw a punch at my buddy Dave while we were in an after hours shit-show known as Drai's. The argument was over who was talking to the hot waitress first, even though both men were married at the time. It was a weird scene and made everybody uncomfortable – but no one more than I, suddenly forced to break up a fight between a friend from college and a friend from work. My first thought was, "Why would a married guy even hit on a waitress?" Now, eight years into my marriage, I totally understand. It has nothing to do with actually sleeping with another woman, it has to do with seeing if you can still flirt. It has to do with seeing if you still have GAME. It has to do with hoping that your slight post-wedding weight gain and thinner hairline hasn't affected your desirability to someone of the opposite sex. It's why my grandfather held the country club waitress around the waist while ordering a pastrami sandwich and why my stepfather recently told a hostess at a Mexican Restaurant to "bend over, he was driving her home".

I can't make this stuff up.

On the flip side, the same goes for my wife and her friends. The women who spent their bachelorette weekends at the spa now have similar thoughts about what they would have done differently. I asked my wife what the biggest difference would have been from her wine tasting weekend. Without hesitation she said, "There would have been a lot more cock." I am so glad we're married.

Yesterday, Nick's brother sent out an official group email to the bachelor party. Turns out, he rented a cabin in Big Bear and wants to spend the time hiking, barbecuing and drinking local microbrews. Nick seemed to applaud the situation, and even sent out a follow-up email stating, "Thank GOD we're not doing it in Vegas!" I suddenly slunk low in my desk chair. What? No Vegas? What are we gonna do in the woods, trust-building exercises? Fishing? Pinning Webelos' badges on each other? Fuck that.

My one shot at redemption was shattered, my ego deflated. I replied to the email by saying that I had a "family thing" to do that weekend and I couldn't make it. After all, if I'm gonna go camping, I'm taking my son and daughter with me. I don't want to go play "Ookie-Cookie" with nine dudes I barely know in a cabin in the woods. To tell you the truth, I was horribly disappointed in Nick. I even emailed him and told him so. I told him that someday he'd look back on his bachelor party and want a redo. He'd want the strippers and the drugs and the precarious situations. He'd want a memory of a final throwdown together with his friends that tarnished humanity as we know it. I urged him to change his plans and go to Sin City. Reno. Even fucking Laughlin. His stance was strong; Big Bear it was.

So, I'm no longer going to Nick's bachelor party. The sad thing is, after Nick, I don't have many single friends left. The one wild card is my younger brother, who is still unmarried. If I can convince him to go to Vegas, I might have a shot at reclaiming my manhood. Then again, he's an outdoorsy guy, so a Big Bear situation might present itself again. Nonetheless, until he gets engaged, I will be forced to celebrate my adulthood with my children, going to the park, the beach, and the mall for recreation. I will get my kicks running on a treadmill rather than "making it rain" at a strip club, cheering on YMCA youth basketball teams rather than playing Quarters from a barstool.

And if all else fails, there's always Yogurtland.

The Freestyle

A week ago, I got into a freestyle rap battle.

Now, I know this is not something that a 37-year-old father of two should ever be admitting to, but for some reason last Wednesday night I felt a burning desire to join an intimidating rap circle and try and drop some dope-ass, quick-minded, funny rhymes on some totally unsuspecting strangers.

If there is ever a moment in my life I could take back, it is this one.

Standing out in front of the Smokehouse restaurant in Burbank with my wife and another couple (whose kid is in the same kindergarten class with our son), I decided to make my way into this "cypher". I suddenly turned from "the bearded weirdo who always drives the soccer practice carpool" into "the drunk dad from the kindergarten class who thought he was Eminem".

Let me back up here a minute. See, I used to be a rapper. That is not a typo. I didn't "wrap" presents…I RAPPED. I recorded a few CD's and everything. I had skills. A future. A following.

I know, laugh it up. My outside appearance is deceiving; I am white, fatherly and pasty. I wear basketball shorts and t-shirts 90 percent of the time for "comfort". I occasionally have undissolved Rogaine foam in my hair. I am not intimidating at all.

But believe it or not, at one point in my younger life I was a bona fide record deal–having, somewhat admired freestyle rapper, arguably one of the best in the world. I could rhyme like Dr. Seuss on a mushroom trip. I could think off the top of my head faster than 99 percent of the improvisational actors I have encountered. I appeared in a film or two brandishing my talents. I used to perform my skills live with bands in nightclubs, at late night parties, and at sketch comedy shows. I garnered mad respect. People would come up nightly and ask me, "How the hell does your mind think like that?"

I bet you're wondering how this all started…

In 1987, if you had asked my mother what career she thought I'd pursue as a young man, based on the thousands of dollars I made mastering Jose Canseco and Mark McGwire's signatures she most likely would have said "professional autograph forger." (A near-arrest at the local baseball card shop in 1989 ended that career.)

She might have wished I would follow my father, a doctor, into medicine; but a "D" in chemistry my sophomore year of high school stifled that dream. (I even cheated. And I still got a D.)

I may even have been able to make a living in the courtroom, brandishing my gift of gab in front of honorable judges while trying to convince the jury that the defendant was not even in the country when the crime occurred; but to me, law school was for the geeks who couldn't talk to girls at junior high parties. Or make them laugh at summer camp. Or rap their way into their pants.

"Yo Melissa/ I wanna kiss ya/Take off your dress and I won't dismiss ya…"

The first time I made a rhyme up about a girl was in eighth grade. Her name was Melissa, and we were at Dana Restival's Halloween party. Everybody knew I was the best rapper in school – and after I dropped those lyrics on her in front of a crowd of people, she proceeded to follow me around the party for the rest of the night. Around 9:30 we snuck away, and shared our first kiss near a saguaro cactus in the Tucson desert. It was sloppy, but unbelievably perfect, everything I had ever imagined. In my mind, Melissa was going to be my girlfriend. I thought I had it made. She ended up letting John Coates, the school hesher, feel her up on the school bus a week later.

Back in the 1980's, if you were into rap music, it made you unique. I had a partner in crime named "Ryan the Rhymer" (now a dentist in Tucson), and together we comprised the tightest white-boy rapping outfit at Townsend Junior High School, a two-man wrecking crew known as "SO FRESH". I wore African leather medallions to school and sported those 3rd Bass/Dwayne Wayne flip-up glasses as a way to seem more "intelligent". We wrote raps and performed at talent shows, and were laughed at for not listening to cheesy-haired cock rock like Poison and Slaughter. Back then, we were the musical outcasts because we liked Beastie Boys, Shinehead, and Boogie Down Productions. Then one day, we won a student council election based on one of our raps called "Do it for the School!!!" After that, we were no longer considered out-of-touch losers.

The first time I performed at my high school was in the ninth grade, when a kid named Eric Tiberon challenged me to a rhyme-off. He was black, and had the entire school behind him for the sole reason that he had a high-top fade like Kid from Kid 'n Play. When I accepted his challenge, people were somewhat scared for me; but the final parking lot battle went a little differently than expected. Eric basically recited Eazy-E's classic "Eazy-Duz-It". I made up a rap about how much being in ninth grade sucked.

Eric rapped about cars and girls, neither of which he had at the time.

I rapped about being beat up by a high school bully named Jason and getting a C in geometry. I remember my verse well:

"School sucks, I get up so early/ Bully named Jason always looking so burly/ Said I looked like a freshman girlie/ stuck my head in a toilet and gave me a swirlie…"

Yeah, I know it was Will Smith-ish, it wasn't hardcore or gangsta, but it was funny – and the people loved it. So much so, that Eric and I became friends after that, even going to see *Ghostbusters 2* together just to hear Bobby Brown's new song "On Our Own". (Still holds up today. CLASSIC jam.)

High school was still an awkward stumble through athletics, music, girls and experimentation, but hip-hop music was always a staple in my life. I rapped over "Humpty Dance" break beats at high school dances and earned my juice on the dance floor busting out the Running Man, the Roger Rabbit and the Butterfly to songs like "The Choice is Yours" by Black Sheep during my junior prom. By my senior year, I thought I could make a legitimate rap album.

And then *The Chronic* came out.

Dr. Dre's album changed my life; suddenly, dancing wasn't cool anymore. My style of rap sucked, and whatever street cred I had amongst my Tucson brethren went out the window. I was Vanilla Iced-out. Squashed. 187'ed. Ignored.

At the time, I was surprised at how little I cared. In fact, it was a relief to know that my rap career had ended. The following fall I enrolled at USC in Los Angeles. I was engulfed by West Coast G-funk, but also expanded my taste into other areas of music as well. I picked up the acoustic guitar as a means to get laid, and even started my first band with my pal Jason, the only other kid I knew who could play more than three chords. We were called, sadly, "Two College Freshman".

We were at USC one year removed from the famed LA riots of 1992. West Coast rap dominated; but I no longer wanted to be a rapper. When I compared the number of girls I got when I rapped versus when I did an acoustic cover of "Your Bright Baby Blues", I realized who I really wanted to be was Jackson Browne. Especially after legends 2Pac and The Notorious B.I.G. were murdered, I knew a 3.8 GPS-having son of a Jewish doctor wasn't exactly cut out for the rap game.

I ended up making ends meet in college by DJ-ing and emcee-ing fraternity parties and weddings, eventually branching out into Bar Mitzvahs. But by the time the late 90's rolled around, and I found myself making the acquaintance of musicians in bands like Matchbox 20, Paperback and even 'NSYNC, I noticed that everybody still always talked about the newest rap music out at the time. Puff Daddy, Mase, Nelly – you name it. This was the music of the time, and even the biggest non-hip hop stars I knew were obsessed with the genre. I'm not sure where it happened for the first time, but I was around some guy who began freestyle rapping. He was decent, but his trite choice of lyrics and lack of originality made me consider attempting my own rap. I jumped in. He nodded along, probably unimpressed, but nonetheless enjoying my effort. When I was done, he gave me a fist bump and walked away.

I did it again with the guys from 'NSYNC. Living in Los Angeles in 1998 meant I had a lot of young friends who were trying to act, sing, dance, direct, or produce. One of my buddies had grown up with Chris Kirkpatrick (probably best remembered as the guy Eminem threatened to beat up in a song in 2000), the dreadlocked "bad boy" of 'NSYNC, the most popular boy band in the history of the world. Chris and I would get drunk together and end up in some random hotel room with a bunch of girls and background dancers and rap producers at two in the morning. Inevitably, after thirty Heineken bottles littered the floor and a few joints were passed, people began rapping. I started stepping in. I started getting the laughs, making up rhymes and ultimately the tightest flows of any so-called "rapper" hanging around these after parties. And it was easy to rhyme "Get stoned" with "Joey Fatone."

Around 1999, I ended up in the Standard Hotel with Dr. Dre. He was surrounded by 300-pound bodyguards, his personal "blunt-roller", and a crew of slinky women who looked like they were in En Vogue, along with about ten wanna-be rappers. That night was the first time I was actually afraid to rap in front of somebody in nearly ten years. In fact, after witnessing three saggy-pantsed douche-nozzles try to rap Dre's ear off, I decided that perhaps my rap future was a pointless joke. I guess I always knew what I did in hotel rooms with my friends was more of a party-trick and less of a career choice, and it didn't bother me. I had no interest in becoming a professional rapper. I was committed to having fun and getting laid and occasionally jumping onstage after ten drinks to freestyle along with my friend's band at their Hollywood club gigs. We were 25 years old, wasted and happy and sleeping until noon. We were naïve and convinced that fame and success was just around the corner.

One of my friends, a hip-hop dancer for the local rap station Power 106, began calling me "Zachariah"; I immediately took on the moniker as my rap handle. "Zachariah, the Rhyme Messiah". I would go around any room and rap about what people were doing, wearing, drinking, you name it. I never thought it would lead to anything but a few free drinks and some laughter.

And then somebody offered me a record deal.

A girl I had fooled around with, Lisa, knew a rap producer named "Cookie" and she arranged a meeting for us at the Skybar on Sunset Boulevard. I wasn't sure what I was going to do during this meeting, but I put on a cowboy shirt and fluffed my hair up to Lindsay Buckingham–heights, hoping to seem marketable and charismatic.

At the time, nobody in LA had any type of haircut but a short spiked boy-band thing, so my wild Jew-fro gave me a little edge. It somehow made me seem a bit more reckless, maybe even dangerous, if only in that "I don't give a fuck" drug-addict look that you see outside of Venice Beach grocery stores.

At the Skybar, with Lisa next to me, "Cookie" told me to order a beer. Lisa bragged about my ability to freestyle as Cookie stared me down; he took a long pull off his beer and asked me to "do something impressive".

I froze. Was he serious? What was I supposed to do, recite some lyrics? Tell him some song ideas? Instead I rapped off the top of my head to the cocktail waitress.

"Come here now for a second Miss Blondie/ Any chance you wanna get on me?/ You live in LA? I'm from Arizona/ Do my boy Cookie a favor – another Corona?/ Don't mistake this – I can't fake this – you're so hot for a waitress/ Do ya have fake tits? I cant tell/ That's alright, I still think yer swell/ My name is Zachariah, how do I look?/ Trying to rhyme for this dude named Cook/ I'll steal yer heart like a bona fide crook/I'll take yer naked photos and put 'em in a book/ So let's just let this relationship bloom/ So here's the key to my hotel room…"

The waitress smiled. Cookie looked at me and said, "I want to capture THAT in the studio."

I made out with the waitress that night.

A week later we were in Cookie's studio, known as "LeftSide." I had written a song in Las Vegas with my friend Jacob called "Runnin' Shit" about two guys who slept with girls, traveled to Mexico and Vegas on random Wednesdays, got high, and drove really nice cars. In reality, we were both Southern California Bar Mitzvah DJ's. The last time I had been to Mexico was with my mother on a family Christmas vacation (typical Jewish trip – Mexico over Christmas) and I drove a 1989 Dodge Lancer.

To top it all off, I was unable to do anything in the studio that night – but SUCK.

The studio was a small rented office space off Slauson and La Cienega. Cookie hooked me up with a producer named Warrior, a master of the MPC 3000. We smoked some weed, made a beat, and put together a silly rap song full of impersonations, bad jokes, and pop culture references. It was called "Come On", and I was convinced it was my ticket to the big time. Cookie started marketing me to record companies as "if Eminem hung out at Dawson's Creek".

I should have quit right then.

I put out an EP on Q/LeftSide Records – and it went triple plastic. Every major label rejected me and I ended up with a closetful of 3,500 CD's. One of the songs on the album, "Other Side", featured a friend of Cookie's named Stacy Ferguson. Today she's known a little differently, as Fergie from The Black Eyed Peas. I never thought she had much of a future. She had a voice from God, but so did a lot of girls. What did I know?

After LeftSide folded, I ended up starting a country rock band that dabbled in hip-hop. We had a little local success, but not much more. Once I got on TV, I was able to convince the folks behind the scenes to let me record some songs for nearly every show. Today, those residual checks amount to roughly 63 cents a year.

I also recorded a bunch of stupidly silly comedy rap songs about cartoons I'd like to f*%&, "White People Problems", and the TSA. I have released a few CD's on some small labels and I have been hired by over two dozen companies to write and record rap songs for their products, from Levi's to Netgear. So I guess, technically, I once called myself a rapper; but I certainly never took it seriously. And now that the style of rap is so different, I have no idea how to imitate lyrical geniuses like Lil Wayne and Drake. I'm still stuck in that Will-Smith-meets-Skee-Lo style. It's the kind of rap that gets zero respect.

***

According to my calculations, it had been nine years since I truly "battled" somebody. A battle between emcees usually involves insults, braggadocio and clever wordplay, performed off the cuff and under a lot of pressure. A lot of rappers suck at this, but for some reason I was always able to come up with quick rhymes. In fact, I have never lost a battle in my life; other fools have claimed they out-rapped me, but most of them recited something I could tell was written beforehand. I was strictly improvisational.

Freestyle rapping is like working out. You need to do it all the time or you get rusty. Rarely do you take nine years off and then step up to the microphone and sound like Rakim. But last week, following a few glasses of red wine, I thought I was back in the Skybar in 1999.

The three dudes standing outside of the Smokehouse restaurant in Burbank were sharing a joint and rapping about Maybachs and "stackin' chips". The valet parking attendant took our ticket as I caught one of the guy's eyes. I guess in the 90's you would call what he was doing "mad dogging". I would normally run from any large crew of wasted black dudes in a parking lot at eleven at night, but that night I felt the need to jump into the rap battle instead. Maybe it was because he kept staring at my wife and obviously commenting under his breath about her. Whatever it was, I felt like I needed to say something. I took a step towards them.

"Punk ass bitches get stitches like snitches/rub you out like a genie, grant ya three wishes/ Im a killa, son, drinking Miller, son/All the tracks on my album dope, no filler son…"

I heard the guy's rhyme. Not bad, but I knew I could hang. I sort of stumbled over as my wife failed to pull me back and stop me from entering the cypher. As I walked up, they noticed me and rapped about my approach:

"White boy stepping up, what the fuck he want/ Gonna kick him in the dick if he pull a stunt…"

The three guys laughed uproariously. I started getting nervous. I heard my wife gasp. The other couple we were eating with immediately signaled for their Volkswagen Touareg to be ready to drive off should I get into a street brawl or something. I slipped up to the crew of rappers.

"Are you guys rapping?" I asked, realizing I sounded like the fat pledge in Animal House asking the frat brothers if they were playing cards.

They burst out laughing. I thought I was doomed.

"Yeah, you wanna step in?" a large man with a diamond encrusted grenade-chain offered.

"Well, I actually freestyle…was hoping to get in on the cypher."

More laughter. They punched each other's shoulders and leaned their heads against one another.

"Are you gonna put your doggie bag down first?" one of the guys asked.

I looked down. In my hand was a plastic bag of leftovers with a red bow around it. I looked like the schlub I used to make fun of when I was younger. The out-of-touch chump who was taking home half a New York Strip and three pieces of cheesy-bread after a double-date night. I knew the only way out was to rap. I began firing.

"Yo - I take a bag of leftovers from the smokehouse/ you can continue with your jokes now/I'm broke now – so I have to eat this for breakfast/ When's your next concert? Put me on the guest list/ I spent my weed money on my wife's gold necklace/ That's her over there, she's got the best tits/ I've ever seen and they ain't even fake/ We live in a house over in Toluca Lake/ I bust freestyles in only one take/ Put the kids to bed stay up late and get baked/ and I know I look lame and somewhat old/ You guys look like a younger De La Soul/ But my wife's calling me to get the car and go home/ Because she don't want me to catch another cold/ So I'm out – thanks for giving me time / I doubt any of ya'll can defeat that rhyme!"

I stepped back and took a breath. Wow. I had dropped 16 bars in front of a crew of three hardcore hip-hop heads who probably took rap music more seriously than I ever had…and I had held my own. I was proud and I looked back at my wife and the other couple, who were stone-faced and somewhat impressed. "Wait until I tell my son about this!!!" I thought to myself.

And then one of the guys began answering my challenge. His name was Black Angus.

"Yo, white boy – your white noise aint right boy/ yeah I see yer wife, she no longer tight, boy/ cause I did her last week/ in the back seat of my Jeep/ Did it in five seconds without a peep/ while you was asleep/ getting kids ready for school/ I gave her my tool and took a piss in your pool/ Smoked your bullshit weed/ pulled it indeed/ Killed you like Drago did Apollo Creed/ Planted a seed – inside her – you mind?/ Now you wonder why your kid looks like mine?/ Don't step into my circle unless you bring skills/ go home to your anti-anxiety pills/ Watch whack white TV like that show The Hills/ and keep being a sucker and paying yo' bills/ You a dumb-ass honky who cant rhyme for shit/ Now go back to your minivan before you get HIT."

The crew cheered. Our friends' Touareg sped off and I was silenced. A terrifying chill, like one I've had on airplanes when we hit some odd air pocket that scares even the flight attendants, engulfed my body. I was smoked. Forget winning a freestyle battle, I had been pulverized, insulted, dissed and clowned by a dude outside of a steakhouse that I would probably never be able to go to again. I faked a laugh, and tripped backwards towards my wife and our awaiting car; which, by the way, is NOT a minivan.

"How'd that go for you?" my wife asked as we raced off into the Burbank night.

"Uhm, not well," I said.

After five minutes of complete silence, I uttered my final words on the incident.

"Why'd they have to be so mean?"

I sulked into my home. Being a little buzzed, I turned on the TV, only to be humiliated further by each commercial starring Andre 3000 or Ice Cube. It was a cold bucket of water to the face, reminding me that I am at best a decent freestyler, in no way cut out to be a professional. Bottom line? I am too much of a pussy.

The next morning, I pulled out the leftovers from the Smokehouse and considered making a steak and egg omelet, the one indulgence I was going to allow myself. But when I saw that half of a New York Strip in the bag, it brought back too many bad memories from the night before. I tossed the meat in the trash and settled for a bowl of Trader Joe's 'Honey Nut O's' instead.

That afternoon, the new *Rolling Stone* arrived.

Fergie was on the cover.

The Tailgater

"What year do you think I graduated?"

The tipsy, long-legged freshman blonde I was talking with staggered back a few paces. She took a sip from the Coors Light beer can that she had been smearing with guacamole residue for the past five minutes and flipped her silken hair back over her shoulder. She hiccupped, adjusted her neck, and gazed up at me. She answered.

"Uhhhm, I don't know, 1980?"

"1980?" I responded. "What! No, I'm only 37!"

"Oh my God," she said. "You're my stepmother's age."

I didn't cry. I didn't have to. I just shook my head and walked away. I walked back towards my tailgate section, where ten of my closest buddies from my days as a student and football fan at the University of Southern California stood inebriated and buzzing with excitement, longing for those glory days of yore. Back when The Notorious B.I.G. was still alive and Sublime played our fraternity parties. Back when my major and the quality of my fake ID was all that mattered. Back when tailgating on campus was for old, creepy men trying to get some Alpha Phi to show them her tits, while we were the future generation, heckling the 40-year-olds for showing up with beer bongs.

1980. Really? Are you serious? I was FIVE! I couldn't believe it.

I slouched over to the cooler and kicked the ground. Even before I sat down in my beach chair, my friends could tell I was upset.

"Yo, Z, what's up?" my buddy Spencer asked.

"Oh, nothing. Just that that freshman girl over there thought I was 54 years old."

Tailgating is a time-honored tradition amongst my friends and I. Once a year we pool together about a hundred bucks a person and blow it on beer, cheap food, and football tickets to see the USC Trojans play at the Los Angeles Coliseum. Most of our day is spent ogling young college girls on campus, drinking, throwing footballs around, and reminiscing about all the amazing times we had in college; basically, trying to pretend we are 20-years-old again. In fact, in the fifteen years since I graduated, I think I've maybe sat through one half of a live football game. Keep track of the score? As far as we're concerned a win is a good thing, but most of the times we had done this before we were so wasted by kick-off time we didn't feel it necessary to even go to the actual game.

The fact that this freshman girl thought I was nearly twenty years older than I am reminded me of how naïve and unworldly we are in college. Students think they are doing great things, studying interesting subjects, and having meaningful relationships, but in reality, most of them are using those four years as a crutch to get by without facing the real world of work, marriage, children, and bills. Most of them think there are jobs waiting beyond the campus with six-figure paydays and keys to executive bathrooms. Even I was guilty of this. Back in the 90's, I thought that by studying broadcast journalism, I'd be able to rely on sports broadcasting as a "back up job" should things not go my way within two or three months of graduation. Instead, what I realized many years later is that my degree meant jack squat. Based on the success I have had using my major thus far, I might as well have majored in bongwater.

Saturday, September 22nd started out the same as every other tailgate day my friends and I had participated in. We loaded up on greasy food, found the few USC memorabilia T-shirts we owned, and barely scoffed at the $25 parking fee for a local structure by campus. (The fact that I had no problem dropping 25 bucks on parking, whereas I am angrily putting off my son's $25 youth soccer registration fee because I think it's too high, makes no sense to me.)

My old roommate Spencer wore a red, collared USC shirt. My friend Neil chose a 50-0 USC/UCLA score recap shirt and a black USC baseball cap. Our pal Riley was wearing a #55 hockey jersey, if only to start a conversation with superfans. As for me, I had spent the previous week trying to manufacture cheap t-shirts that we could sell on campus to stupid college kids that read: "IT'S BANG A FRESHMAN DAY!"

The printer wouldn't let me make them.

We made it to campus around 9:00 in the morning, and had cracked open cans of Miller Lite by 9:03. We strolled around our old dormitories and hang-outs, noting that the school had seriously upgraded everything since we had left campus back in 1997. That was back before the Staples Center was built and the surrounding campus became desirable. When it cost me $425 a month to live with three dudes in a fully shag-carpeted condo; a dismembered female body had been found in the grocery store dumpster across the street a year before we moved in. When the school was an affordable $25,000 a year. (I took out roughly $92,000 in student loans. Fifteen years later? I've paid back 18 bucks).

A sprawling quad had replaced once rusted volleyball nets, heaving with shirtless Greek system Gods and Goddesses. Old dormitories looked like Westin hotels, and the on-campus bar Traditions, which once sat about 20 people (ten comfortably), had recently been transformed into a cavernous USC-themed booze playground that resembled an ESPN Zone in Las Vegas.

Yes, the campus had changed as much as we had. And nearly everything I did that fine Saturday made me realize just how far removed from college I truly was.

The first questionable thing I chose to do after being mistaken for a 54-year-old was pull out a bottle of red wine. Not some $7.99 Trader Joe's bottle of cheap Pinot swill called "Nosedive" whose label features an actual nose skydiving, but a legitimate 1994 Shafer Cabernet Sauvignon Hillside Select. I'm talking about a $152 bottle that I bought at a wine auction in 2010 for half the price. A bottle you either save for an anniversary or lose when your teenage son and his friends find the wine cellar in the basement. Having pretty much shunned beer recently for my new red wine obsession, I figured this was a terrific bottle to share with my best buddies from college on a grassy patch of tailgate in lieu of Miller Lite # 19…oh, how wrong I was.

"Dude, seriously?" Riley snorted as he watched me use my Reef flip-flop with the attached corkscrew to get the bottle open. "Red wine? Are you gonna take your bra off when you drink it?"

"It's 97 degrees outside!" Neil offered.

"What is that, two-buck Chuck?" Spencer chortled.

When I explained to the guys that it was, in fact, a significant bottle of 1994 Napa Valley gold, they laughed, cracked another beer, and continued taking stealthy cellphone pictures of the crew of scantily clad Kappa Kappa Gamma girls playing wiffle ball thirty feet away. As I poured my glass I knew it was a wasted bottle, but I figured I'd try to enjoy it anyway.

"That ball was outside!" I yelled at a fraternity pledge who had been acting as the umpire during the wiffle ball game. Before I could get into a Billy Martin-type argument with him, he looked over at me and sized me up. I knew what he was thinking: *Great, another old, jerk-off alumni trying to be funny around the sorority girls.* After I tried to put on my best "I was once on ESPN" broadcaster voice and call some humorous play-by-play, I quickly realized just how out of place I was. 37-years-old. Married. Two kids. Somehow still thinking I would be able to get the female response I used to get back in college; my nickname then was "The Oil-Rigger".

The fact is, my two-and-a-half-year-old *daughter* is closer to her freshman year in college than I am. When I graduated college, the majority of today's freshmen were three- and four-years-old. I was already taking PROPECIA for crying out loud. Today? My six-year-old son's kindergarten costs roughly $25,000 a year. Typical USC tuition now starts in the $54,000 range. You also need about 1,000 points higher on your SAT to get in, far better than the 1050 I slid by with in 1993. (I've decided that my kids are going to University of Phoenix by the way. Online.)

So there I was. Sipping a $50 glass of wine from a red plastic cup, watching five tank top-sporting, wiffle ball-playing frat dudes with names like "Troy" and "Carson" try and work their magic on a crew of sorority girls. The same kind of girls I would have once easily convinced to come "power hit" a bongload with me in my apartment as we listened to Blues Traveler's *4*. Girls who I once would have taken CD shopping on a date. Girls who think I graduated college in 1980.

After a few drinks, I took a trip to the Porta Potties near the Von Kleinsmid Center, where I had once aced a few classes on gerontology and gang relations. I remembered it well.

The Porta Potty lines were long and the sun was blazing hot. I knew that there were bathrooms in the building somewhere, but my memory being a little hazy, I decided to just use the filthy toilet and get back to finishing my wine before getting down on some Costco barbecue rib dish Riley was seasoning. So

I stood there in line along with about 75 other older people awaiting a chance to relieve themselves.

After about fifteen minutes or so of inching closer to the front, a young kid around 21 came bounding by. Apparently the new college fad was to Duct-tape together multiple beer cans into some sort of beer-saber so you can defeat a Sith Lord by the end of the tailgate. When he handed his girlfriend his beer-saber and strolled past the line we were all standing in, he looked directly at us and laughed. His next words hurt the most:

"Standing in the Porta Potty line? What a bunch of NOOBS!!!"

Noobs? No, sorry. You can never call me a noob. I used to know every toilet on campus. From the row of thrones near the bookstore to the hidden former-darkroom toilet in the journalism school basement, I was the king of finding a bathroom at USC. This little fucker just called me a NOOB?! I was on *Attack of the Show*! For three years! We practically invented the term "noob". I planned on confronting the prick when he came back and demanding an apology.

He was back in three minutes, his bladder emptied, as I still stood in the never ending line from hell. He grabbed his girlfriend and his saber and went off to chase more college glory. I ended up peeing in a honey bucket that had a USC-logo'ed baby diaper smeared on the floor. Perhaps I was a noob indeed.

Even though the tank top kids had had to leave the game to fetch their frat masters some more beer, the Kappa Kappa Gamma wiffle ball display was still going strong. Somehow Neil, a one-time NorCal 5-tool baseball prodigy, had been recruited to throw practice pitches for the girls as they giggled and whacked plastic balls towards Tommy Trojan. I managed to sneak myself into the game as the catcher, hoping for just one blissful Lingerie Football League play at the plate. As one girl after another stepped up, I began ribbing them the way Yogi Berra might have back in the glory days of baseball.

"What's your major?" "Ever date a Jew?" "Need a date for your spring sorority formal?" "Nice grip — lucky bat…" It went on and on. Until this blonde girl named Jessa took her gum out of her mouth, turned to me, and told me to shut the hell up.

After we somehow got three outs, we demanded that we got to bat. Jessa – who told me she was a senior – made her way to the mound and began stretching like Jennie Finch before a College World Series softball game. I got scared. We all did. Still, the experience had turned us into college kids again. And we all loved it. For some reason these girls had let us into their game, and we were happy to be the creepy old guys playing nine innings against an infield of short skirts and memories. It was old-timers day at the ballpark and we didn't give a FUCK.

Then, Jessa yelled that she needed a drink. You have never seen a crowd of more desperate, overweight men run towards a girl than you did that afternoon to Jessa. It was like a bench-clearing brawl where we all rushed the mound – but with beers in hand. She decided against a beer and went for a sip of my glorious wine; I was thrilled. As I broke down the currant undertones, floral notes and chutes of ember in the bottle, she took one sip, spit it out and said, "That's the worst thing I have ever drank in my life!"

My buddies nearly fell down laughing.

Down 5 – 0, I finally got up to bat. Riley had led off with a double and Neil had singled him over to third. I had a chance to drive in a few runs here, and like most men who play sports around a bunch of women, I really felt like I wanted to do a little better, become that high school jock I never was. Make up for batting .117 my final year of Little League. All I knew was that I refused to strike out, that it would be the worst thing in the world. I had one motive. I needed to go yard.

Jessa readied for the pitch and leaned back on the mound. After throwing me two dastardly sliders – which I had fouled off – I knew she was coming with the heat. I looked at Neil, and he knew she would throw it as well. It was then that I decided to go for the laugh once more.

"Throw me a cock-high fastball," I said.

Jessa laughed. In fact, everybody laughed. A comment I had stolen from a Sports Illustrated writer discussing locker room quotes had prompted more uproarious laughter than we had experienced the entire afternoon. And right there, in the southern California sun, I felt like I might have been back in college once again. Running the game. Getting the laughs. Having the right major and preparing for some crazy booze- and pot-filled after party in my apartment. I cracked my neck and stepped in the batter's box.

I was so energized, I felt like the time was right to regain my manhood. It was time I got a second opinion on when a hot young college girl thought I had graduated.

Jessa looked into her sorority sister's glove as I heckled her one more time. She shook off the sign.

"Hey, Jessa," I said. "What year do you think I graduated?"

She paused and looked back at me. She made eye contact. I gave her my best "Luke Perry" smolder – forgetting that this girl had no fucking idea who the hell Luke Perry even was. She responded.

"Uhh, I dunno – 1984?" she said as the confidence drained from my body.

She threw me a cock-high fastball.

I swung at it…and missed.

I Got Next

I got dunked on this morning.

Yeah, posterized. Embarrassed. Juked. Lit up. Dusted. Shook, took, and left for dead. Jammed on by a 20-something human helicopter in the YMCA basketball league I recently joined. It was pretty damn humiliating, especially since my wife and six-year-old son were on the sidelines. This 6'6" athletic specimen, with arms like boa constrictors and the vertical leap of a Madagascan cheetah, decided to gloat while high-fiving his teammates, shouting "Take that white boy!" in my general direction. Our coach Jerome called a time out and quickly informed me that I wouldn't be coming back into the game for a while. I understood. I sat on the bench and hung my head against my 2004 Arizona Wildcats basketball shorts and wiped heavy beads of sweat off with my towel. I slowly looked over at my son, who turned to his mom and asked her why Daddy got taken out of the game. Ever the subtle parent, my wife informed him, "Your dad just got annihilated."

When I first joined the Hollywood YMCA, it was on my doctor's orders. My family history had a lot to do with it – and his main motive was to get my cardiovascular activity up and my cholesterol down. Since basketball has always been my favorite form of exercise, I chose the Y because the courts were full of older players with no other motivation than a little activity and some fun. The majority of the guys I encountered on Tuesdays and Thursdays were in their 30's and 40's, wearing some sort of knee brace or elbow support sleeve. They put up long threes, blew easy lay-ups and spent half the game talking about the Hollywood trades and other silliness, killing time as their kids tooled around the clubhouse downstairs. Rucker Park this was not.

After hanging around the sidelines for twenty minutes or so, I was invited back in to play; I quickly put up a dazzling 6 points, 3 rebounds and 2 assists in a

21-19 thriller of a pick-up game. In my mind, I was back to those glory days when I used to school young Jewish guys in the "Stephen S. Wise Temple Basketball League". Back when I made the Junior Varsity team at my high school and actually had the ability to dunk a basketball on a ten-foot rim. (OK, I only did it twice, but I *did* do it.) Back when my life was simple and easy, when the only thing that mattered was which pair of Air Jordans I would save up for to try and impress hot Tucson girls enough to actually consider me a potential prom date.

Nowadays, the last thing I remember dunking is a celery stalk into a Bloody Mary. Those Air Jordans are long gone. So is my vertical leap. And according to Facebook, all those hot Tucson girls now have teenage kids and have been divorced twice on average since high school. So in my mind, scoring 6 points in a YMCA game was the equivalent of winning an NBA Championship. I immediately told my wife that I loved basketball at the YMCA, and I showed up again the next day to take on another set of chumps with my wicked first step and decent mid-range jumper.

Turns out, the Monday/Wednesday game features a totally different crew than the guys who play on Tuesday/Thursday.

My first indication that the competition was on another level was the fact that most of the guys on the court didn't have beer guts. There were dudes even playing shirtless, a thing you only see down at Venice Beach during the summer, and they looked like their bodies had robotic sound effects when they moved. Some guys had basketball tattoos reading "Ball is Life" and "Love of the Game" beneath an orange ball swishing through a net. One guy stood close to 6'10" and practiced drop-step lay-ups while a scraggly Steve Nash-looking kid fed him bounce passes. Another rained in threes from NBA range, shouting out "ALL DAY!" whenever he connected…which was a lot. Finally, a shredded swing-man named DeMar threw down an Isiah Rider through-the-legs dunk during a fast break. I quickly turned and headed towards the door, opting to run on the treadmill that day instead.

Little did I know, DeMar would be the same guy who would later dunk on me; but let me back up for a second and explain how I even got invited to play in the YMCA league in the first place.

Back in the summer of 2008, I was covering the famed "San Diego Comic-Con" for *Attack of the Show*, a TV program I was hosting. The convention was a nerd party of epic proportions, and I took full advantage of every open bar in the Gaslight District, including a party where celebrated Ohio State star and Portland Trailblazers number one draft pick Greg Oden made an appearance. Being one of the only basketball fans in the entire city that night worked to my advantage, and Greg Oden and I spoke for a good twenty minutes before he was whisked away by a publicist for some interview. After he left, a geeky fanboy tapped me on the shoulder and asked me if the seven-foot Greg Oden was Samuel L. Jackson from *Snakes on a Plane.*

In November of that year, I was inspired to get myself into shape. I read that Nike had announced the release of the new Greg Oden Power Max basketball shoe and the minute I had read about it, I knew that would be my shoe. After all, Greg had been so cool at Comic Con, and I was convinced he had a Michael Jordan–like career ahead of him. He was exactly the kind of role model I needed to reclaim my past basketball prowess. The day the shoe was released I took a trip up to the Topanga Canyon mall, where I dropped $130 on a pair of Nike PE's with "Oden" very prominently stitched across the laces as well as the back of the shoe.

Five years later, as you may or may not know, Greg Oden is considered one of the biggest disappointments in the history of NBA basketball, right up there with Sam Bowie, Joe Barry Carroll, and Michael Olowokandi. Yes, a BUST. His injuries have left him sidelined for all but 23 games or so, and the guy drafted after him, Kevin Durant, has gone on to become arguably the best player in the NBA. As of this pressing, Greg Oden is currently coaching basketball clinics in Oregon. I hope he invested his money wisely; otherwise he might be hanging sheetrock in a few years.

Unfortunately, his shoe is the only basketball shoe I own. Basically, I refuse to ever pay that much money for a shoe again, and since I never really wore his model that much anyway, it is in fairly great condition. A year ago I tried to see if it would sell on eBay, but as the only other model on the website was a "Buy It Now" offer for $9.99, I figured I'd just play ball in my Oden's until they fell apart. (By the way, you can buy 100 – yes, 100 – Greg Oden Topps rookie basketball cards for $3.99 on eBay right now.)

So, I am stuck with my Oden's and there's a small part of me that actually kind of enjoys the irony of owning them. It's like having the film *Gigli* on Blu-Ray.

The treadmill I run on at the YMCA faces the pathway between the basketball courts and the water fountain, so the players come out every twenty minutes or so for breaks. They have never noticed me running before, but that Wednesday they decided to approach my treadmill following the first game they had played that afternoon. I wasn't sure why…until they called me by my shoe.

"Yo, Greg Oden!" one wiry dude yelled just as I hit my nine-minute-per-mile stride. "Come off that treadmill for a second, man!"

A little intimidated, I kept running.

"Why?" I asked.

"We wanna ask you a question," he responded.

I pressed pause on my iPhone and stepped off the treadmill. I had run 1.2 miles in ten minutes. 151 calories. Meh.

I walked over to the crew of dudes who were somewhat taunting me, like jocks in high school making fun of the kid who played piccolo in the band. Why were they here? What did they want? I quickly found out.

"Where did you get a pair of Oden's?" the leader asked.

As his crew looked down at my shoes, the laughs and taunts continued.

"Whaaaat?"

"Nice choice, bro!"

"Really? Oden's?"

For some reason, I was facing ridicule for Greg Oden's injury-prone career, as if I had been Greg Oden. It didn't make any sense. So, as I have always tended to do, I made a humorous jibe about the situation.

"Yeah, I got these when he was the biggest prospect in basketball, alright? I could afford one dope pair of shoes, and I fucked up and chose these, OK? Whatchu think, I can afford a pair of Kevin Durant's?"

The guys laughed. They high-fived me. They made me feel better. They were funny, and seemingly down to Earth. And then, maybe as a kind gesture (or just as a way to see how terrible a basketball player I was), they invited me to come get into a quick game of pick-up hoop in the main gym.

A lump appeared in my throat…could I hang with these trees? Was my game on their level? I mean, if my shot was on I might be able to put up a few buckets, but if my nerves got the better of me, I risked the horror of becoming known as the "Greg Oden of the YMCA".

Painted into a corner I said okay, and tightened my $130 shoes and walked out towards the basketball court, convinced that I was about to get schooled by a bunch of guys who probably played Division I, NBA D-league, or even overseas basketball.

The tip-off was the first sign that I had entered some ring of Hell. After Fez from our team won the tip, a guy named Derrick told Fez that the ball wasn't thrown up "evenly", and a huge shit-talking session ensued for the next three minutes.

I had seen these trash-talker games before. Basically, a lot of guys call fouls on every play and their opponents complain about the calls. The games take forever to finish because nobody ever actually plays, they just spend most of the time jawing at each other. It sucks to play in and to watch. After we held a re-jump ball, nearly every two or three trips up the court ended in a heated exchange.

"Hell, no, THAT'S A FOUL!" yelled a guy called Jay Reezy who was covering up his embarrassing air ball.

"Foul… and one!" screamed Joelle as his ball clanged off the rim.

"Man, get yo hand off my dick!" shouted Lorenzo, after I cleanly swiped the basketball from his hands. Yes, it was clean, but he accused me not only of the foul, but of molestation. They took the ball back and scored on sheer intimidation factor on the next play. The reality of YMCA pick-up basketball had set in. When Lorenzo yelled, "I'ma KILL you motherfucka," to our sideline coach Jerome after he called a traveling violation on a jump shot, it vaguely reminded me of that scene from *White Men Can't Jump* (a film that director Ron Shelton actually envisioned while playing on the selfsame courts) when Marques Johnson's character went to his glove compartment to get a gun to settle a dispute. I believe the line was "I'm gonna get my other gun and I'm shooting you AND him…"

Whatever the case I was scared, and I did my best "hide around the three-point line and pray that nobody wants me to shoot" routine. Woody Harrelson, I was not. Amazingly enough, I did attempt one three-pointer…and somehow nailed it.

As the game wore on, I notched up another bucket on an inside pump fake that got the team yelling "Nice one, Oden!" As I spent a minute jogging back on defense, I couldn't help but notice as a guy named Red flew by me and converted a lay-up against an older center whom I had recognized from Tuesday's game. As I threw the ball in, I jokingly told him, "You should've called a foul." He smiled and passed the ball up to the front court.

The game turned out to be the longest pick-up game I have ever played. There was more chatter, more arguing, more fouls called, more shit-talking and more disagreements than I have ever seen, even in my six-year-old son's Junior Lakers League. It was like playing against spoiled teenagers, and I wanted to fake an injury just to not play anymore. Still, I was with the big league players at the YMCA… and I was hanging.

When the buzzer sounded, we were shuffled off the court for the next crew of five. We had lost 21 – 17. Even though I only scored five points, I honestly felt like I had played better than some of the trash-talking intimidators who had been there dealing handfuls of smack to their opponents. I was inspired, and convinced that after a little practice I might be able to step back in to bang with these big boys. Following the game, when Coach Jerome invited me to sub on their YMCA league team the following Saturday morning, I knew I had proven myself as somewhat of a baller; I was shocked and flattered, and I responded to his request with a foolish exclamation of "Dope!"

I immediately felt like an idiot.

I came home and informed my wife that I had made the team…sort of. I mentioned that I was invited to substitute for another player and that I needed to be on my A-game on Saturday morning. My wife, an actual high school All-State player, seemed impressed. The stage was set. I had a league game on Saturday! No news yet on if I'd be starting, but I was nervous as shit.

I decided that a quick pick-up game in the Jewish Basketball League wouldn't hurt my confidence either.

Back in 2000 or so, I was a terror on the courts of the Jewish Basketball League. My old roommate Mike and I had been a lethal inside-outside combination, and even though I would enter most games sweating beer and whiskey from the night before, our Stephen S. Wise Matzah Ballers defeated the Temple Hess Kramer Lions handily for three years straight. Many of our players have gone on to Hollywood success, others are long gone from the city, but some are still playing. I always knew in the back of my head that if there was a place to regain my basketball confidence, it was the Jewish League, a run I specifically refer to as "Heeb Hoops".

Thursday evening, I rolled into the Michael Milken gymnasium wearing a Carmelo Anthony jersey, cradling a Vita-Coco water. My old roommate Mike was still running the league. Not much seemed different, except for the fact that Mike was now sporting a Rip Hamilton face mask that he had been fitted with following his fourth broken nose. Shockingly, the nose-break is a very common Jewish basketball injury.

Mike gave me a silent nod as I surveyed the competition before warming up. Convincing myself that these young players had nothing on my storied Jewish Basketball League career, I shot a few jumpers, ran some drills, and worked on my left-handed penetration – a skill I had been lacking since those JV days back in high school. By the time I was allowed to get in the run, I was on top of the world. And it showed. I shook Gabe Friedman on a crossover that gave us a two-point lead. Mike fed me a pass and Jordan Mogelwitz fell for my pump-fake and ended up watching me bank in a 7-footer on his left. Even Raphie Spiegel bit on my daring long-range three that tied the game at 16, before my old homeboy Mike crossed-over a college kid and put us up by a bucket. Mike and I ended the run with a classic give-and-go, punctuated by his three-pointer that won us the game. Mike and I celebrated, exchanging awkward 37-year-old dap handshakes and chest-bumps. I had made nine of our points; Mike, twelve. It was 2000 all over again. We even smoked a joint in the parking lot afterwards and made stoned plans to form a team that had a shot at winning the coveted "Dead Sea Cup" in the fall. It was amazing. I got home, showered and went to bed, convinced that on Saturday I would be running YMCA regulars up and down the court from the first whistle.

Oh, how wrong I was.

The YMCA league resembled the All-Valley Karate Championship from *The Karate Kid.* Some dudes were mad-dogging any potential challengers like Johnny Lawrence did Daniel LaRusso. Teams were stretching and warming up like it was the Final Four. Guys with prison-sized muscles ran suicide drills and barked orders at their teams. I recognized DeMar the shredded dunker working on his through-the-legs jam during a lay-up drill. Some other players from the YMCA were there too, representing different branches. We were Hollywood, but there was also a Downtown crew and an intimidating Westside team. Most of their players looked bigger and more confident than I felt. Even my teammate Fez seemed to be in the zone, dishing out chest passes to our team before noticing my arrival and demanding I let my wife and kid know they had to remain outside the gym until the sidelines were opened up to the public. I immediately knew this game was a bad idea.

I did not start the game. In fact, I "rode pine" the entire first half, doing what I do best: mocking people. I reverted to the 13-year-old clown who developed his ESPN-worthy broadcast voice on the bench as the 10th man on his junior high championship team. I regressed into the sophomore who spit funny commentary from the bench as my team lost by 29 to Marana High School. I became the stoner kid from college who skipped our fraternity basketball tournament due to a mushroom hangover. I was simply not taking anything seriously.

"Jesus, I've seen better jumpers hooked to the battery of my car," I announced.

"He couldn't hit air if he was skydiving," I offered.

"He's got more turnovers than a bakery," I joked, terribly.

I went on and on. Until two minutes before the half when our coach, Jerome, informed me that our leading scorer Gary Vernon had sprained his ankle. I was in at small forward, and that I "better not fuck it up."

Luckily, with a minute left, I handled my own. I was able to guard their sharp-shooter somewhat easily, at least for 60 seconds, and when the halftime buzzer sounded I hustled to the sideline, winking at my wife and son, knowing we were up by eight points.

At halftime, I prayed that Gary would be able to return. Unfortunately, he told Coach Jerome he was out. I was summoned to start the second half and I told him I was ready to answer the call.

The second half was reminiscent of the YMCA pick-up game I had witnessed a few days before. Smack was talked, play was delayed, but luckily the presence of referees helped move the action along. A minute in, I got passed the ball for the first time. I looked inside, but had no outlet. I took a few dribbles around the perimeter before handing the ball off to our point guard. He drove the lane and was quickly rejected…the ball bounced back towards me, wide open outside of the three-point line. Now, in my life, I have performed for crowds as big as 1,500 people. I have no fear of the spotlight; I embrace it. So of course, at that very moment, I did what any lifelong performer would do: I froze.

Like a statue. Good old DeMar ran up and swiped the ball from me before beasting towards the other side of the court where he easily converted a tomahawk rim-rocker that brought the crowd to its feet. I was suddenly the worst player on the court. I felt that familiar lump rise in my throat. Sure, I could perform music and comedy in front of 1,000 people, but when 18 folks including my wife and son were standing on a nearby sideline, I had no idea how to execute anything. The floodgates of failure had been opened.

DeMar went on a scoring tear, scoring twelve points in under five minutes. Our eight point lead became a four point deficit. 21 points would win it, and it was now 17-13.

I felt the crowd getting into the game. I looked towards my bench and saw Gary glaring at me as if I had stuck his pet kitten in a microwave; it was not exactly the support I was looking for. As I tried to juke the opposing team with some cross-pattern routes I remembered from high school ball, I was checked by a player and felt like I had run into a concrete wall. I staggered back slightly, a bit dazed but conscious, before looking up to see Fez's missed three-pointer bounce my way. I turned my back towards the basket if only to imitate the Lebron James and Magic Johnson moves I had grown up worshiping, but lost confidence when I sent a lazy pass over the lane, intended for a guy named Rick Cahill. Unfortunately, that pass was read with precision by DeMar.

I made the mistake of chasing him down the court. By the time I had come close to catching up to his superhuman speed, he was already 39 inches in the air. I leapt up as well, and thought for a second that I might have a chance at slapping the ball out of his hands. Instead what happened will forever be known as the worst sports moment of my life.

He threw down a one-handed ogre-fuck of a dunk. The ball thundered off of my head. It ricocheted against the back wall and sadly crept towards the exit of the gym before pausing against a stranger's bag. Almost as if it had been shot by a hunter with a cross-bow, it did everything but deflate and bleed to death. Coach Jerome called a time-out.

Within a few minutes we had lost 21 – 13. I looked over towards my wife and son. She had already taken him out of the gym to spare him from the carnage. Our players threw water bottles at the bench and cursed to each other. They asked Gary about his ankle and offered him fifty solutions to heal it. The rest of the team exited quickly, avoiding eye contact with me. Before Coach Jerome could leave the gym, I yelled out at him.

"What time's game next week?"

Jerome looked back to me and offered, "You don't have a game next week…"

As DeMar disappeared to the sidelines and put on a pair of Beats by Dre, I stood up and made my way down to the locker room to shower. As I walked inside, I could hear many of the members talking about DeMar's dunk and how incredible it was. When I passed them seated tightly in a circle, I noticed they were watching something on one of their phones…the dunk. Someone had filmed him taking flight and obliterating the rim at my expense. I hastily tried to tip-toe out the door, but before I could escape, one of the guys called after me.

"Yo, dude!" he said. "Quick question for ya…"

I stopped in my tracks and turned around, afraid of what low blow he would send my way. Anticipating the worst, I took a deep breath and awaited sure insult and humiliation. Finally, he spoke.

"Are you wearing Greg Oden's?"

I cracked a meek smile and threw my towel over my shoulder.

"Only until I can afford a pair of Sam Bowie's," I joked.

The guys chuckled, probably because they felt sorry for me, but it was enough to show that I wasn't taking any of this stuff that seriously.

As they replayed the dunk over and over, I slipped out the door and called my wife. She answered the phone by saying, "I'm sorry."

We spoke for a minute about everything but the game. What we needed at the store, what time the kids needed to be at practice, even what Netflix we wanted to order. It was a nice distraction from my embarrassing moment on the court.

After I said good-bye to some of the other players, I looked around the YMCA and quietly announced my retirement from the basketball league to nobody in particular.

And then I went upstairs to run on the treadmill.

A Pirate's Tale

I just came to the sad conclusion that I would have made a lousy pirate.

My entire life, I have been infatuated with legendary late 17th century buccaneers and their high sea adventures. I have fantasized about discovering imperial treasures, establishing small island colonies comprised of sexual heathens, and washing down slabs of roast Zebu meat with never-ending rivers of Carribean rum. I've imagined sailing into tropical ports clad in worldly fabrics, a silken scarf billowing out from beneath my manicured vest. I've envisioned a cutlass tucked into my waistcoat belt, complimenting a gun or two hidden upon a hip to be used only in case of ambush. I have seen fair virginal maidens awaiting me in every port. Yes, for thirty years, I have dreamt of *piracy*.

I have always imagined myself living this life, thinking that perhaps I was born at the wrong time. I was meant to be a sea-beaten swashbuckler possessing a Dread Pirate Roberts-like combination of wit, trickery, swordsmanship, and romance; a mysterious villain with a heart (and a chest) of gold, gorging myself on intercontinental coffees and licquers. Forever eluding capture, living my life on the winds until the proper time arrived when I would lower my mainsail, trade my beloved ship for gold, and retire to live like a king in some sun-drenched slice of paradise. I have visualized spending my final days bearded and leathery, awash in Key West swells, living off the fruits of my labors. The sea has always called my name.

So when my father-in-law invited me to join him on a fishing trip, I accepted immediately.

We are very different types of men. We have not necessarily spent a lot of bonding time together; in the quest for a connection between my wife's father and myself, I have tried a lot of angles. Unfortunately, it has been hard to find any common ground.

Back in 2001, when my father-in-law and I first met, he had never been to a major league baseball game. I had never fired a gun.

He had never written a song or a short story. I had never flown an airplane off of a carrier in the Pacific Ocean.

He scoffed at the use of profanity in film and television. I had just written a song called "Cartoons I'd Like to Fuck".

I sensed it was going to be tough to find that much in common.

Over the years, I have discovered that my wife's father is a true man of the sea. Following a storied 35-plus years as an airline pilot, the events of 9/11 forced him into early retirement. Bored with the sky, he was delighted to start focusing his attention on his true loves: sailing and the ocean. He celebrates the big blue and all that comes with it, everywhere.

For instance, his house is decorated like the inside of a Santa Monica seafood restaurant. Old fishing nets line the kitchen walls, complete with plastic lobsters caught in their webs. Vintage ship wheel clocks keep time at 26 different spots in the den. Small circular windows are placed on the port and starboard side of the living room. In one room, shark's teeth serve as a makeshift picture frame for his wedding photo. Above his bed is a thrift store painting of Captain Cook inspecting a compass and a map, and his shower curtains are seven foot tall lug sails that he ordered on eBay.

Friends who have visited sometimes refer to his home as "Red Lobster".

I will say that I absolutely respect his passionate worship of the sea; it is his true mistress. When we visit him at his house in Washington state every Christmas, I often find him avoiding the shrieking outbursts of my children by stepping outside, making a fire, and longingly staring out across the open water, where an undiscovered land of opportunity might await him. I would not put it past him to believe that somewhere on that horizon lies an island with a river of frozen pina coladas, buried treasure, and a posse of randy mermaids prepared to satisfy his every perverted need.

In short, he too harbors dreams of being a pirate.

My father-in-law had owned a beautiful sailboat for many years; as a younger man, he took his family around the world and home again on it. But his post-retirement dream was to refurbish another boat into the ultimate dream cruiser. His plan was to take all of us around the world in four years.

In 2001, he bought the boat. Following some terrible storms and unfortunate circumstances, he sold that boat for half of its value nearly a decade later. It had never left the dock.

However in 2012 he finally got a vessel he deemed worthy. It is a beautiful boat, with sleeping room for eight, common hang-out areas, and gorgeous deck space. He spent the majority of the past year sailing it from Maryland, between some Caribbean islands, through the Panama Canal and up back towards Seattle. It was his dream journey. When I heard that he was on this fabulous trip, my old brigand dreams were rekindled. I harkened back to my obsession with colorful pirate captains like Robert Culliford, Blackbeard and Calico Jack. I dreamt of a night on that boat, searching high above for the Andromeda Galaxy through my spyglass while cosmically spaced-out on aged Puerto Rican spiced rum.

In March my family received his postcard from the island of St. Croix, illuminating us on everything we were missing. As I sat on my couch, firing up another game of *Wii Wipeout,* I realized that he was absolutely right. And I was jealous. My father-in-law was out on the high seas, island hopping and fishing for his dinner, while I was spending my life challenging my six-year-old on the treacherous *Wipeout* 'Big Balls".

Luckily, one night during last year's holidays, my father-in-law and I happened upon the fantastic film *Hornblower* on television. I had a few glasses of wine and immediately fell into the story. It was fascinating. He informed me that he had the entire mini-series (on VHS, nonetheless) and we tackled all eight parts within the next three nights. After that, we went through *Master and Commander, Dead Calm, Treasure Island* and the *Pirates of the Carribean* collection. It was then that I inquired about possibly joining him on his next worldwide journey.

"Why don't you start by coming out with me tomorrow?" He offered. "I'm going to set some crab traps and head to Port Orchard Bay to do some fishing."

My eyes lit up. Crab traps? Fishing? A boat? I know it wasn't exactly commandeering a massive English Man-of-War, but it was a start. I figured I would get my sea legs, catch some fresh dinner, and be back by sunset to drink some beer and cook fish while counting the sailboats in the harbor. My first pirate adventure awaited me. I felt like one of those career deckhands who spend their lives in the bars of port towns like Bremerton awaiting a three month job on an Alaskan fishing vessel, where they might make enough on the icy water to stay in booze for weeks.

My wife was her usual supportive self. "Don't come back with a peg-leg," she requested.

I slept well that night anticipating my maiden voyage on his boat, *The Great Orca II,* where I would ride the Pacific Northwestern waves until I was christened first mate. I awoke at dawn to pack, ready to head out on the open water.

Before we set out, I took my journal with me hoping to find some inspiration. I also fastened my guitar to my back (knowing that pirates always appreciated a good sea shanty) and tucked my headphones into my jacket pocket. As the sun rose, I watched my father-in-law put on a set of rubber pants and some Merrell boots as I laced up my Converse All-Stars. I arrived in the kitchen ready to embark on our little journey with my guitar and iPad. He arrived wearing a knit beanie, holding a pair of pliers.

"What are those for?" I asked.

"In case we hit something and one of your teeth pops loose."

I froze. He smiled.

"So, what's your sea name gonna be?" he asked me.

"Excuse me?" I said. "Sea name?"

"All my passengers must create sea names for themselves when we are out on the water. You know, aliases. I always go by 'Captain T'."

I thought about it. A sea name! Cool! I knew my pirate name had to be something legendary, with a little flourish and a hardened edge. Something like "Black Pistol Bluebird McCoy".

Knowing that there was a "Pirate Name Generator" on the internet (look it up), I quickly logged on and typed in my name. Sadly, their suggestion wasn't the heroic adventurer name I had imagined. On the website, it read:

"Yarr olde name be Zachary Selwyn. But we'll now call ye: *Pants-Down Darius.*"

Pants-Down Darius?

My wife laughed. So did my mother-in-law. I demanded to re-enter my name, but it was too late. The new sea name had stuck.

"Hey, *Pants-Down*," Captain T yelled. "Don't bring your guitar unless you want it to get ruined."

(For the record, when my father-in-law typed in his name, he was anointed *Pirate Laszlo the Ochre*...lucky bastard.)

Now I have been fishing a number of times. However, most of my deep sea adventures happened somewhere down in Cabo San Lucas, and involved an unlimited supply of Modelo Especial and a drunk Mexican pontoon boat captain named "Suarez". I figured this little trip would be the Pacific Northwestern version of that; basically a short little booze cruise into Port Orchard Bay.

As I slipped on the wet step ladder that hoists a passenger into his boat, Captain T called back towards the house where my wife and kids were waving good-bye from the back porch.

"Better stand in the 'widow's walk' now," he chortled. "He might not make it a nautical mile!"

Widow's walk? Sailor humor, I figured. I stepped into the cabin and drank some coffee. It was cold outside, but I figured the sun might come up soon enough for me to catch some open-sea rays before catching our lunch and heading home. I lay down to try and catch another ten minutes of rest.

Five minutes later we set off from the dock, and I found myself alone on the water with my father-in-law. It suddenly dawned on me that if my daughter was to ever marry a man like me, I would do everything I could to find a way to "accidentally" push him off of a boat into arctic waters. I immediately became paranoid that I was on a boat trip not unlike the one "Big Pussy" made with Tony on *The Sopranos.*

After getting out of the inlet waters that surrounded hilltops scattered with Bainbridge Island mansions, we settled into a nice stretch of slightly bumpy water where I figured we might drop some crab traps. As it turned out, we were early. Captain T informed me that we were just stalking until the tide came back out. I looked at my watch. It was 8:13 a.m.

"What time does the tide come back out?" I asked.

"Around 10," he responded.

The next hour was remarkably the most relaxed I had been since we had arrived for the holidays five days prior. Captain T and I played cards, looked at pictures on our iPhones, and talked about what type of fish we wanted to have by the time we got back to shore. We both snacked on some almonds and popped open bottles of Amber Lager while playing the card game "Casino".

We discussed my children, our careers, and how good life would be once we emptied his crab pots and reveled in the abundant shellfish found below the surface. There was no *SpongeBob* on TV, no diapers to change, and no wives to harass us about drinking beers at 8:30 in the morning.

"Are there laws about how long you have to be sober before flying a plane?" I asked.

"When I flew for Pan Am the rule was 8 hours bottle to throttle."

"What about when you're on a boat?" I inquired.

"Probably something like, 'Don't get into trouble, drop anchor when you see double'."

It was by far the hardest my father-in-law has ever made me laugh.

It might not have been piracy, but it was a deep hang. I enjoyed it so much I began doing the math in my head, trying to figure out how much property I could get in a small Seattle waterfront town if I sold my house in Hollywood. Probably a *shitload.* And a decent boat. And I could own and operate a small fireworks stand on the side of the road near the Suquamish Indian Reservation. For 45 minutes, I was truly considering this massive life change.

And then the storm broke.

The Pacific Northwest isn't exactly known for its dry weather. In fact, they average only 23 days of sunshine a year, explaining the high suicide rate and tremendous coffee production. Sometimes when we visit, we get lucky and only have to withstand a small patch of overcast skies and minimal rain. Unfortunately, this afternoon was not one of those times.

Sheets of water began to pound the *Great Orca II*, forcing us to cut our engine and enclose ourselves in a plastic sheathing to protect the engine room. I helped button down a few knobs, but I began to get a little concerned when, following a heavy pane of rain, I heard my father-in-law cursing at something from below deck. Being that he was a man who found *Mary Poppins* to be morally reprehensible, I was amazed at his sudden vulgarity. The man I had known for eleven years had become the re-incarnation of the revolting British pirate Bartholomew Sharp.

In his home, the word "damn" demanded punishment.

Out here on the water, the words "fucking cockshit" suddenly became acceptable.

"Something wrong, sir?" I yelled below deck.

"Stay up there *Pants-Down*," he yelled back.

I leaned against my seat and did my best to ignore the boat's nauseating rocking. I dumped the remainder of my beer over the side.

"We got a breach in the hull," he yelled. "Get me my black toolbox, NOW!"

I panicked. Not knowing where he stored it, I frantically searched in the state room before coming across what I thought was a black tool box. I brought it down to him and he slapped it away.

"That's a goddamn tackle box, Zach!"

So much for only using our sea names.

"Stay here and apply pressure to where this leak is coming through, got it?" he said.

I nodded and applied pressure on a tarpaulin that he had fastened over a small crack in the boat's bottom. Water was seeping in fast. Assuming the hole didn't get any bigger, I figured we had three hours before we would be re-enacting scenes from *The Perfect Storm*.

When Captain T got back down, he cursed at the scene and thrust me out of his way. He threw open his tool kit and removed some puddy-like mold and went to work. I sat there, frozen for what seemed like 20 minutes.

"Anything I can help with?" I offered.

"Go upstairs and radio the Coast Guard…we might be stuck out here tonight."

Back above deck, I fiddled with the radio but had no idea what the hell I was doing. When I couldn't get any response I simply garbled "SOS" into the receiver. I figured we were done for. We were barely five miles from his house, but we were in the middle of nowhere. Looking around, I did not see another vessel in sight. At least I was going to fulfill one part of my pirate fantasy: being buried at sea.

In the world of pirate adventures, rarely did a buccaneer get a chance to enjoy the treasures he pilfered. Most pirate galleons were besieged by disease, starvation, dehydration, and long, terrible droughts of immobility. Ships would fail to catch wind and be stranded in the middle of the ocean for days on end, making life hell for the crew. Very few pirates got away with anything without dire punishment. Should a pirate be captured, his life became even more unpleasant, spending years holed up in a dank, smelly, cavernous prison chained to a wall with only a chamber pot for company. If one was lucky enough to get pardoned, he would more than likely end up penniless and ruined. The lucky ones died of scurvy or dehydration. Many hung from gallows to welcome incoming ships, warning them about the perils of piracy. Basically, making out well in the world of 17th and 18th century piracy was about as common as moving to Hollywood and becoming the next Hugh Jackman. It took a strong will to be a pirate, spending a treacherous nine months on a boat hoping for one miraculous ship capture and a raid that would make you rich; the toughest ones stuck it out.

I had been at sea for a grand total of two hours and five minutes and I was ready to abandon ship.

About ten minutes after I had given up on the pirate life, Captain T came back up to the bridge and asked me for a towel. When I handed him one, I noticed that he was soaking wet and smelled like the open sea. He was shivering something fierce, and his droopy face beneath his wool cap made him look a little like a drenched sea lion.

"Well, I got the leak fixed," he said.

I nearly got up and hugged him. I couldn't believe it.

"Any word from the Coast Guard?"

"Uhh, no," I replied. "I wasn't really sure how to call them."

Captain T picked up the radio and spoke into it. When he did not receive a response, he calmly holstered the radio and sat back in the Captain's seat.

"Looks like we might have to tough it out and get back home through the storm," he mumbled.

As the wind raged on and the boat rocked back and forth, I found myself a victim of seasickness. Vomiting over the side of a boat in the middle of the ocean is a wonderful experience, let me tell you. Especially when the captain recommends aiming *into* the wind so that it doesn't land on any leather boat cushions.

Captain T straightened out some things that had come off the walls before fastening nearly everything down and telling me to hold on to anything I could find. He flipped on the engine and guided the boat around.

"Anything I can help with?" I asked.

"You can get us a couple of beers," he said. "This is gonna be a rough re-entry."

For the next three hours, I watched my father-in-law in his element. Whereas I had spent the afternoon scared for my life, he was fighting Mother Nature like Captain Kidd guiding his ship from the shores of Madagascar back to New York Harbor. Captain T was magnificent. He vanquished every challenge the water threw at him, relishing each chance he got to steer clear of an oncoming swell or ride through an air pocket with ease.

No wonder this guy flew planes for 35 years, I thought to myself.

It was a true mark of his bravery, one that reduced me from a valiant wannabe pirate to a lowly stowaway, longing to warm my feet by a fire while flipping through 298 television stations.

He dipped over waves and squinted through the wind like a cast member of *Deadliest Catch.* He navigated wearing nothing but a cap, rubber jacket and a long sleeve shirt, icicles forming on his beard. Meanwhile, I was in nine pairs of long johns and two sweaters.

About two hours later we had made it safely back to the dock, where I helped tie up some lines and put out ship bumpers so that we wouldn't scratch the vessel. As I walked up the dock towards the house I looked through the windows, noticing the familiar positioning of my family. My wife was on the couch. The boy was wielding a lightsaber by the kitchen table, and my mother-in-law stood cooking chili. I stopped for a moment and watched this Rockwellian scene, waiting for Captain T to come out of the boathouse so that we could congratulate each other. After all, we had survived the storm! We had made it through! We were men of action, true sea dogs. This was quite possibly the closest we would get to being pirates our entire lives.

I knew our story wouldn't be as impressive once we relayed it to our couch-dwelling family members, but it was still something to be proud of. We had gone out fishing, fixed a damaged hull, and returned home with all of our limbs. For the first time in awhile, I was elated. I felt like a *man.* I couldn't wait to get back inside, crack a cold beer, and impress my wife and kids with my tall tale of heroism.

I opened the sliding glass door that led out to the boathouse and wiped my feet on the mat. I stood in front of my wife and kids, awaiting some questioning and subsequent hero-worship. After all, when pirates would return home after time at sea, they were lavishly praised and decorated by their loved ones. I was hoping for a similar treatment.

"How was it, *Pants-Down*?" my wife asked.

I now understand why my father-in-law always stares out at the water.

The Newark Shower

I took a shower in a bathroom sink at the Newark airport this morning. I am not proud of this fact, but there was no other choice. A job relied on it. A job that could lead to worldwide success and financial stability. A job that might change my life forever. In other words, this was a job deemed worthy of bending over a dirty sink in the United Airlines terminal.

I never understood how people did it. You know who I'm talking about: the guy in the terminal bathroom who brushes his teeth or changes into a suit while standing over the very sink you are trying to wash your hands at. The dude flossing his teeth and spitting in the trashcan. The traveler practically shaving his chest in the bathroom before he flies across country… I hate these people. I mean, did the hotel you were in the night before NOT have a shower? Do you have to take headshots upon touching down in your next city? Why in God's name are there people washing their hair in airport bathroom sinks?

Here's why it happened to me.

A TV show had offered me an opportunity to come do a screen test for their program and was flying me to New York City. Since this was a last minute thing, I was placed on the earliest flight out of LAX on a Wednesday morning. I would arrive mid-afternoon at Newark airport and be whisked away to a midtown studio to audition on the same day. So basically, I would be traveling on the plane, landing, brushing my teeth in the Lincoln Town Car they were providing, and arriving at the studio an hour later.

Of course, I woke up at 4:45 for the 6:00 a.m. flight.

I figured that without a jet pack, there was no way I could make this plane. My dreams were slowly fading with each tick of my broken alarm clock. Luckily I wasn't checking bags, so I rousted my kids out of bed and made my poor bedraggled wife drive me at 95 miles-per-hour to the airport. What is usually a 45-minute drive in Los Angeles traffic miraculously took us 23 minutes. I stepped off the curb at 5:16 and watched my wife flip me the bird as she drove away.

I pushed my way past the security lines claiming that my wife was in labor across the country. The kind TSA agents let me pass and I somehow slipped into seat 23B at 5:52 a.m. I took a minute to smell myself, and caught a faint whiff of red wine and body odor seeping through my denim shirt. I didn't care. Once we took off, I was just happy to be on my way to a screen test across the country that I almost slept through.

The flight was uneventful aside from the screaming child four rows up, making me realize just how lucky I was to be traveling solo for a change. In the tweeted words of @JohnQuaintance, "*When you're flying without your kids, EVERY seat is first class.*"

I leaned back my chair and shut my eyes. He was right indeed.

I spent the final two hours of the flight studying up on the script I had to memorize. The wardrobe was "upscale casual". I was wearing a pair of Mandals. I realized I would have to clean up and shop before stepping into the audition. For one, I smelled. I was also unshaven, bleary-eyed, and wearing denim on denim. I looked like Jay Leno on a Michelob Ultra bender.

The passengers filed out of the plane and I followed suit. I managed to snag a *XXL Magazine* with A$AP Rocky on the cover just to give me something to read in the Town Car. From past experience I knew that New York City car services normally offer horrifying reading material in the backseats like *WristWatch Magazine* and *Hobby Farming Quarterly*. (Last trip to New York I read the entire "poultry issue" cover to cover.)

I scratched my scruffy beard and stretched as I got into the terminal, deciding to go face myself in the mirror for the first time that day.

I may not have checked any bags on the plane, but I certainly checked a few beneath my eyes. I looked like Joaquin Phoenix during the filming of *I'm Still Here*. I had an uneven beard bordering on homeless, and now sported a seemingly permanent crease from the right side of my forehead down to my chin line from sleeping on the flight. My hair was sprouting in a thousand directions and resembled Gene Wilder's after a dust storm, and at least two new zits had decided that this was their day to blossom on my neck.

I stepped back out to take an inventory of the shops around me, and for the first time in many spent in airports, I had a revelation. Airports need to be more like truck stops.

Truck stops are the perfect place to relax when you are on a road trip. You can get *everything* at a truck stop. I am not just talking about fast food, sodas, and snacks. I am referring to the fact that you can stop at a place like Tonopah Joe's (between Palm Desert and Phoenix) and buy everything from low-level trucker speed to a decent "Flying Camel" from a female lot lizard who hangs around the café. Showers are warm and affordable, and they even rent small bedrooms for quick naps. The attached bar is straight out of *Urban Cowboy*; you can get liquored up and lucky before sleeping it off in your truck cab. One of the employees might even fancy himself an outlaw country singer, selling his own CD at the register to prove it. About the only thing the place does not have is WiFi.

Compare that with the modern day airport. Every terminal has its share of bars (which I believe should always be frequented when flying). However as far as personal hygiene goes, the lower-class truck stop has the upper-class airport beat. Sure, you can buy a *Sleepless in Seattle* nightgown in the SEA-TAC airport, but there is no place for you to go to sleep in it.

You *can* however purchase a ten-minute massage in many airports for $15. Having made the mistake of paying for this once, I was extremely disappointed at the lack of pressure applied by the lady rubbing my back. It may have been because she was less-than-thrilled with my hygiene, or more likely because she was texting the entire time. And showers? Forget it. The closest you will ever get is shoving your head beneath a faucet and feverishly scrubbing the dirt out into the sink with a mini soap as horrified travelers stare at you in wonder.

The Japanese on the other hand have it all figured out. While in the Tokyo airport in 2008 I paid a few Yen to sleep in a drawer-like compartment for twenty minutes before sitting on a toilet while purified water from Mount Fuji water-boarded my arse. I was given a steam room token, and access to a large community sink where one could wash up and refresh before a flight. Finally, I entered the officer's club for a first class meal of udon noodles, sushi, and unlimited beer. The closest I have ever come to that in America was spilling a nine dollar bottle of Arrowhead Water on my crotch at a Chili's Too.

That being said, I had three hours to prepare for the biggest audition of my life. After cruising the five restrooms in the United terminal, I decided that the one farthest away from the restaurant was the safest bet. Big mistake.

Apparently, people prefer doing their business in restrooms far away from the restaurants they are eating or drinking in. Just as I put my foot into the sink to wash it with the stolen bar of United soap, a sordid symphony of flatulence erupted from the three occupied stalls to my left. It was harmonic and ghastly, like the sound of dozens of geese being sucked into an airplane engine just after take-off.

While the folks finished their business, I resumed my sink shower and did my best to attempt a dry razor shave ($6.00 for two blades in the gift shop). I brushed my teeth, put in my contact lenses, and spent the next ten minutes trying to make my hair do anything besides look like it was washed in a toilet. Deciding that my "upscale casual" look would have to be more "Bohemian hipster", I dabbed some shaving nicks with toilet paper and went to meet my driver.

The ride to Manhattan took an hour, and I read through the *XXL* quite quickly. I passed on reading their provided back issue of *Adventure Kayak Magazine* and studied my lines instead. When we arrived, I walked around the block looking for a thrift store; instead I stumbled into a men's boutique where I purchased a $65 dollar blazer that strongly contrasted with my jeans. They had a terrific return policy, so I felt safe that I wouldn't eat the money. I walked around the corner and bounded upstairs to meet the producers of the show.

"So, Zach - you decided to rock 'The Business Mullet', ehh?" the producer said.

"Excuse me?" I responded. "The *Business Mullet*?"

"Yeah, jeans and a blazer. That's what all the fashionista bloggers call it…"

I was mortified.

"Luckily," he continued, "this is a show about gourmet foods – so I don't care what the hell you wear."

I spent the next hour working with co-hosts and casting directors, finding the humor in a script that was altogether humorless. I ate three greasy pork tacos, six different chorizo sliders and a venison avocado quesadilla, describing it all using words like "exemplary", "aromatic", and "mealy". At the end of my audition, I thanked the team and ran downstairs to return the jacket before the store closed; unfortunately, I had missed the window by 15 minutes, and I banged on the door to no avail.

I stepped back into the waiting Town Car, preparing to return to Newark Airport and fly back to LA. It had been a quick trip and I was proud of my audition, but I was also aware that I had sweat through my shirt during my read because I had forgotten to pack my deodorant. Plus, I now owned a terrible overpriced blazer and my stomach was turning like a washing machine over the oil-smothered Mexican-fusion meal I was forced to eat for the TV show.

After putting down two glasses of cheap red wine at a sports bar known as "The Foul Pole", I boarded my plane at 10:00 that night and settled in for the return to LA. I got into a conversation with the gentleman next to me, who kindly bought me a few beers. When the plane's turbulence kept the bathrooms off-limits for the majority of the trip, I was forced to hold it all in. By the time we landed at LAX, I was desperate..

I walked into the bathroom and peed for what seemed like a full minute. As I went to wash my hands, I came face-to-face with a man feet-deep in the sink, finishing up a toenail scrub and hair-combing. I washed my hands next to him before looking his way. He dried off with a wad of paper towels and began to shave in the mirror. As the hair fell from his face into the sink and he braved the few nicks a cheap razor purchased in an airport will give you, I gestured some tissue his way.

"Big audition today?"

Hooked

My son asked me quite possibly the most brilliant and unanswered question in fairy tale history last week during the second act of *Peter Pan* at the Pantages Theater. He was fascinated by the always entertaining Captain Hook and his rambunctious crew of pirates, dancing around singing spiritedly about their notoriety. Just as they finished up another number, he leaned over and whispered in my ear:

"Dad, what was Captain Hook's name <u>before</u> he got the hook?"

I stared ahead at the acrobatic actress spinning around as Peter Pan. I nodded my head a few times, searching for an answer to his obviously simple question…but I could not come up with anything. I was baffled, and also a little amazed that I had never thought about it before. I slowly turned back to him and said, "That is a really good question."

When the play concluded, I asked the other couples we had attended the play with their thoughts on the subject. Some guy offered up simply, "Captain."

No.

A mom said, "His real name is James T. Hook…"

I wasn't buying it.

I even waited around to ask Cathy Rigby, the 60-year-old former gymnast (who had apparently found the fountain of youth and was running the equivalent of twelve miles a night reprising her Peter Pan role) my son's question. Her response? "I never thought about that!"

After buying the boy a 25-dollar plastic pirate sword from the souvenir table, I texted a dad from my son's school I recognized across the lobby. I proposed to him the same unanswerable query: *What was Captain Hook's name <u>before</u> he got the hook?*

No idea. But how badly did you wanna bang Tiger Lily??

I spent the next day searching around the web for the answer. I quickly found out that my son was not the first person to ask this question. In fact, many researchers and Pan-o-philes had given it quite a bit of thought. The best answer, I concluded, came from a novel called *Capt. Hook: The Adventures of a Notorious Youth.*

According to the novel, Captain Hook was born the illegitimate son of a nobleman, "Lord B", and an unnamed woman Hook has never met. Denounced by Lord B, James is brought up by a Shakespearean actress he calls Aunt Emily. When he is fifteen he unwillingly attends Eton College as an Oppidan scholar. James is christened "Hook" after murdering the quartermaster of the Sea Witch, rather than in reference to his iron arm; in the original novel by J. M. Barrie, Hook was known as "Hook" before he lost his hand, so this is one way to explain it.

Intrigued, I decided to order the book for the boy, hoping his pirate research would mirror mine and he'd someday sail me around the Florida Keys upon his million-dollar sailboat. I tracked down a used copy on eBay for $3.99 and was about to type in my PayPal password when a flashing "Warning: Sensitive Material" banner caught my eye. Before I ordered the book, I decided to read some more reliable book reviews.

Here's what I discovered:

The book is apparently filled with "brutality that can be disturbing, human carcasses on a plague ship, whipping and beating, poisonous spider bites, swordplay and fighting, a brutal game with lots of injuries, mistreated and tormented slaves, a sailor killed with a hook…Parents beware this is not for kids younger than 12."

My God. This book was the *Inglorious Basterds* of novels. Needless to say, I didn't complete the order.

When Disney took the *Peter Pan* story and made it a youthful tale of silly children thinking happy thoughts and jolly pirates who scoff when their clothes get wet, they apparently changed the entire character of "Hook". According to some historians, in the early 20th century children were apparently so frightened of Captain Hook that they were carried from theaters screaming as if they had witnessed a murder. I couldn't believe this. My Captain Hook had always been a foppish, moustachioed dandy with a rich baritone who occasionally shot his own crew by accident when fixing his hair in a mirror. According to another novel, *Peter and Wendy,* Hook was "cadaverous" and "blackavised". Two words that to me describe neither Dustin Hoffman in the 1991 film *Hook*, nor the 1953 taco-hatted Disney cartoon character. What does "blackavised" even mean?

Whatever the case, I have decided to find out who holds the legal rights to this character, because I truly want to write a retelling of his dastardly ways. For fun I rattled off twelve pages to get me motivated, and I am now awaiting responses to the 20 or so emails I sent to the *Peter Pan* historians of the world. Why?? I am still *absolutely fascinated* by my son's question. And I figure once we secure funding, we'll get Daniel Day-Lewis to play Hook and Jennifer Lawrence for Peter Pan. Or maybe we'll settle for Russell Brand and that Jordyn Wieber girl who won a gold medal at the 2012 Olympics.

By the way, after hitting Hook's page on Wikipedia, I finally came across a quote from *Peter Pan* author J. M. Barrie where he states, "Hook was not his true name. To reveal who he really was would even at this date set the country in a blaze."

So there you go. My son asked a question that got me researching the true history of *Peter Pan*'s notorious villain; it got me thinking and writing, and I am now in the process of trying to write a screenplay about the origins of Captain Hook. Chances are I won't get past page 50, but I really don't care because at the moment I am inspired.

I guess the point of all this is to remind you to listen to your children. Their innocent questions can lead you down roads you would have never explored on your own. My wife and I decided that we will take our kid's inquiries more seriously and not just shrug them off. In fact, we've begun requiring that at every family dinner our kids ask a question. It's a very fun activity to participate in as we laugh over dishes of pasta and vegetables as I deny the boy another turn on the iPad.

Of course tonight my son asked us a question that didn't quite send me racing towards my computer to research, compose, and write. Instead, he leaned over after devouring a plate of peas and whispered into our ears:

"What happens to you if you eat boogers off of the desk at school?"

I nearly choked on my dinner. Hey, they can't all be brilliant…

The Houseguest

If you ever have a friend knock on your door at three in the morning, smelling like stale cigarettes and Wild Turkey and clutching an overstuffed backpack, my advice is to immediately hand them as much cash as you can and demand they go and find a cheap nearby motel.

Trust me. It might save your marriage.

My old fraternity brother Ray arrived at our front door five days ago and simply asked if he could come in and "talk". He appeared somewhat distraught and bewildered, as if he had just come back from tossing the "One Ring" from *Lord of the Rings* into the fires of Mount Doom. Concerned, I invited him inside to relax for a moment and offered him a leftover tub of my kids' macaroni and cheese. He posted himself on the couch, nonchalantly requesting the remote control because he had to make sure he was "caught up on *Tosh.0*".

It is now five days later. Ray has been casually sleeping on the couch in our family living room as if he is the new family dog. He is not sleeping here because he is just "passing through", nor because his house is getting fumigated or because he lost his apartment in a fire. He is not sleeping here because he lost his identification and can't get on any flights back to his home across the country. Ray has been sleeping here because his wife discovered that for the past few months, he has been boning a 23-year-old cocktail waitress named 'Mystique'.

The minute his wife kicked him out of his house, he filled up a backpack with underwear and a few t-shirts, fired up his motorcycle, and apparently decided he would be turning our family's favorite couch into his temporary bachelor pad. At first it was sort of fun to have an old friend around to bounce ideas off, sip a beer with, and battle on my son's Wii.

Now, it's potentially leading to my *own* divorce.

Even my six-year-old son has begun asking when he is leaving.

Let us back up. See, Ray was the guy in college who never had trouble finding a place to crash, a ride home from a late night party, or a spare set of clothes after he had "accidentally vomited" on his own. He had no shortage of girlfriends willing to pull him through his weaker moments by occasionally lending him a few dollars or buying him Del Taco at two in the morning, and he often slept in the hallway outside my fraternity suite whenever my roommate or I was busy entertaining a female guest. Ray was a drifter of sorts. A surfer majoring is business with a minor in weed sales, a guy who worshipped Bob Marley and vowed to someday move to Calcutta, where he would open a paddleboard shop along the shore of the Hooghly River. When I explained to him that the Hooghly was a waste dump and a public bath for millions of local residents, his response was always the same:

"I'll paddle around 'em, brah!"

As it turned out, Ray always tried to paddle around everything.

He had met his wife Elena while in Greece backpacking. At the time she was 31 – five years older than him – and they hit it off while discussing a Bear Surfboard hanging from the wall of their local youth hostel. Elena was from San Diego and had divorced her first husband after he lost all of their money playing online poker. When Ray presented himself as a potential suitor, he charmed his way into her bed by stating, "The good news about me is that I will always be broke, so I can't blow our money in online poker."

Elena fell for him. Quickly.

Back in California, Elena and Ray moved in together and were rapidly married. I had been a groomsman at the wedding, and even played one of my own songs as the new couple walked down the sands of Pacific Beach in San Diego immediately following their nuptials. The after-party was legendary, commencing with homemade fireworks provided by a few beachcombing Mexican teenagers. I tenderly recall Ray and some other dude dragging me out of the wet shoreline sand at four in the morning, just before the tide washed up against me and potentially swept my liquored-up, bloated body out to sea. The next day I pledged an undying oath to help Ray out whenever he needed me…

And that is why, eight years later, he is lying on my once inviting and spacious sofa doing his best to rearrange our couch cushions with his malodorous, tube-socked feet.

The first night Ray was here wasn't too bad. He didn't drink; he played with my kids and cried to my wife about the stupidity of his actions and how he had lost the only woman who had ever cared for him. We ended up watching some terrible animated film with the six-year-old called *Space Chimps*, and Ray laughed as if he was watching George Carlin in 1970. Ray and my kids shared some popcorn, my wife made him tea, and we decided that the next day we would all head over to the beach together to clear our heads and decide what his next step would be.

Unfortunately, the next morning, his next step was into the Hinano Bar and Grill on the Venice boardwalk.

As Ray drank a few beers to calm his raging mind, my wife took our kids off to play in the sand. I decided to hang out with Ray and be a good friend. To fit in, I sipped a beer or two with him and casually mentioned that he could stay at my place as long as he liked, expecting my polite offer to be brushed away with the guarantee that he would be gone by the next morning; unfortunately, he instead erupted in an ear-to-ear smile.

As Ray refused to take the bait, I became wildly terrified. I realized this had been his plan the entire time. Ray took a large swig of cheap beer from his plastic sup, smiled, and looked at me.

"Dude, that's so awesome. I promise I won't stay longer than a month."

Nearly choking on a peanut shell, I told Ray I needed to step outside for a little air.

"Cool, brah," he said. "I'll get us a couple more beers."

In the mildly cool Venice Beach sunshine, my face suddenly began to redden. Was he serious? *A month?* Who the hell arrives at your door and stays a month? It was like a bad Hollywood movie script coming to life. I prayed to the ocean that Ray would find a way to get back on his feet and leave in the next few days. I even prayed for Elena to take him back. Maybe the 23-year-old waitress had an apartment he could move into… I was understandably concerned. I immediately texted my wife that we both needed to start thinking up an excuse to make sure he wasn't squatting in our living room throughout the month of April.

She promptly texted me back.

Your friend... Your responsibility.

That night, Ray decided he would thank us by making us dinner. After gravely burning two bunches of kale and carrots we had received in our weekly overpriced farmer-approved organic box of vegetables, he apologized and decided to finally just order up a couple of pizzas; starving while witnessing our children go through protein withdrawal, we frigidly agreed.

"Where's the nearest Domino's?" Ray asked before looking at me. "Should we get a *Dominator*?"

The mere mention of a *Dominator* made me smile. Back in the early 90's at the University of Southern California, post-LA riots, the only pizza in the area had been Domino's. Known as the *Dominator*, their most affordable delivery deal was two large three-topping pizzas and a two-liter soda for something like $14.99. Back then, five stoned kids could pool together four bucks apiece and demolish nine slices each before starting on cases of beer (of course not gaining any weight in the process). We basically lived off *Dominators*.

I hadn't even thought of said pizza in nearly fifteen years; Ray's recollection made me laugh, and for a brief second, I considered moving out and getting a place *with* him. Of course, that's when my son piped up.

"I'd rather have Village Pizzeria," he said.

Village Pizzeria is the exact opposite of a Domino's Pizza. It considers itself to be *gourmet* and *artisanal* (whatever that made-up foodie word means). The place claims to use water from New York in their crust recipe and features outlandish pizza toppings such as pears, fontina, Serrano ham, walnuts, nopalitos, cabrales, eggplant, prickly pear leaves, and for an extra two dollars, tarragon.

Before a man gets married or domesticated, a few slices of Domino's, Shakey's, Pizza Hut or Round Table Pizza is not beyond consideration, no matter where you are. Once you are married however, wives introduce 49-dollar pizzas from epicurean places like *Mozza* into your diet, where a sliver of otter skin adds an extra kick to an otherwise dull fontina and venison pizza. Soon, a man forgets about the simplicity and beauty of a dorm room *Dominator*, That night as I stood in front of my old friend Ray, I felt guilty that I had let my kid become so pretentious about his pizza.

Sadly, since it had been nearly twelve years since I stopped eating toxic delivery-level pizza pies, I no longer had a Domino's refrigerator magnet with their clearly printed number handy. Instead, I recommended that Ray call the Village Pizzeria and enjoy the artisanal goodness of a pizza furnished with something simple, like slices of garlic, gruyere, and artichoke hearts.

"How *spendy*?" he asked.

"Uhh, pretty *spendy*," I replied. "Like 25 bucks for a large."

"Forget that!" he screamed as he used my wife's laptop to Google the nearest Domino's.

Fifteen dollars and fifty slices of pizza later, my kids had sworn off of Village Pizzeria forever, claiming that their new allegiance was to Domino's. They hugged Ray goodnight and took a quick bath, asking me why "Uncle Ray" hadn't come and visited before. I told them he only came around once in awhile, and proceeded to pass out next to my son as he fell asleep in his bed. His final words before closing his eyelids were, "Uncle Ray rules…"

My wife woke up with the kids the next morning and told me that Ray had to be gone by that afternoon.

Apparently, during the night Ray had decided to drink our remaining red wine and about nine Stella Artois' from our fridge. He had passed out on top of my daughter's favorite stuffed Hello Kitty toy, which now smelled something like "street hobo". The beer bottles created a miniature glass skyline across the kitchen counter, and an empty pizza box had been turned into an ashtray.

"I hope he didn't smoke in my house," my wife stated.

As we prepped our kids for school, making them lunch and trying our best to conceal the mini transient site that had been left in our kitchen, we whispered in hushed tones as to not wake our sleeping houseguest. My son immediately noticed that Uncle Ray had left the Wii on all night and burned through the batteries on both remote controls. To a six-year-old, this is the equivalent of leaving your car light on and killing your battery overnight. After quieting his screams, we told him to stay out of the living room and he seemed marginally perplexed.

As our kids hopped out at their daily drop-off spot, my wife's demonic squint said it all: *Get that guy the hell out of our house.*

My wife dropped me back at home as she went to the gym, forcing me to clean up Ray's remarkable mess. I tried my best to wake Ray up by clanging his bottles together as I carried the bags to the trash cans, to no effect. The dude was out cold and it looked like he might be sleeping awhile.

I retreated to my office where I answered some emails and played a little mid-90's mix of music that Ray and I had always partied to back in college. From the first notes of "Champagne Supernova" by Oasis, I was longing to be as drunk and rested as Ray was right now. For some reason, the music felt *good.*

When Ray finally awoke around 11:30, he stumbled into the kitchen asking if we had any water. I gave him a 44-ounce plastic *Thor* cup from 7-11 and told him to take a shower and leave whenever he felt like it…the front door was open. Unfortunately, he still saw himself as a houseguest for the next month or so.

As he made some coffee, using a pretentious but tasty Los Feliz-area brand known as Intelligentsia ($22 bags of coffee, like artisanal pizza, are another married affectation), he rubbed his face and calmly asked where we kept our towels. Knowing that my wife would probably be upset if I let my drifter friend use our nice, fluffy Supima© Oeko-Tex certified monogrammed towels, I dug through the back closet and handed him one of my kid's beach numbers, a large and colorful piece of sandpaper decorated with Lego Ninjagos.

He laughed and headed into the bathroom to rinse off.

Around one, Ray decided he was going to need to get something to eat. As I was lucky enough to live within walking distance of LA's "Franklin Corridor", (A pretentious name for my neighborhood as assigned by property managers to the three blocks it encompassed), we walked down the street to a bar/restaurant known as Birds, where young, low-rise wearing girls flocked after their acting classes and thwarted the advances of comedy geeks coming off of their three-week sketch group performance at the Upright Citizen's Brigade theatre next door. I had sauntered down to Birds many times in the beginning of my life in the neighborhood, usually pulling the old "I'll go and get diapers at the grocery store" line before sprinting into Birds for two lightning-fast glasses of Miller Lite from the incredibly cool bartender, Brennan. I often raised a glass with a couple of other neighborhood dads who were pulling the same stunt; we called ourselves "The Diaper Boys". Not exactly a moniker that commands street respect, but as cool as I could get during my children's formative years.

Ray and I sat at the bar and watched *SportsCenter* while eating chicken Caesar wraps. After a Diet Coke, Ray decided a little beer wouldn't hurt either and for the third time in two days, I noticed that he was well on his way to getting sloppily drunk. I sighed and ordered a beer from the bartender as well, but I merely sipped mine.

"Why aren't you drinking, brah?" Ray inquired.

"Dude, I have a spinning class at three," I said.

As Ray shook his head in disappointment, he swirled around on his barstool and began to laugh. It was then that he decided to lay it all on the table for me.

"How did the coolest musician/actor/writer, most ass-gettin' son of a bitch from college turn into a fucking YUPPIE, yo?"

I knew that was coming. I shrugged and hit my beer. This is what had happened: I had fallen in love. Had children. Found it impossible to get out of the house past 9:00 anymore to play band gigs for fifteen dollars and pints of beer at the Hotel Café. I had responsibilities, jobs, bills, tuitions, more bills, tight schedules…I had a LIFE. Sure, I was a little disappointed that I had never become the next Neil Young or Alec Baldwin, but I had become a good father and a creative person, and a very happily married man. I still wrote music, got to be on TV once in awhile, and was able to spend a lot of time with my kids. Unlike Ray, who had never had children, I was no longer checking surf reports for my weekend. I was checking lunch menus to ask my son if he wanted me to make him peanut butter and jelly, or if he wanted to try the parentally demanded "organic kumquat and cheese quesadilla" hot lunch item available at his school that afternoon.

I enjoyed my new life. But that didn't stop me from being envious of Ray's nonchalant outlook on life and the endless possibilities that lay beyond.

"You need a Guy's Day," he explained. "I need to remind you of the man you once were."

"There is nothing that can take me away from the life I live right now," I answered. As it turned out, I was *wrong*.

Ray had a friend who got opening day Los Angeles Dodgers tickets every season. Every April 1st or so, he secured a box seat with an open food buffet and half-price beers. Ray demanded that I attend the celebration with him. April 1st was three days away; I wasn't sure I could commit. He baited me by telling me we could get "close enough to smell Matt Kemp's pine tar". He claimed that opening day at Dodgers Stadium was so full of hot girls that it was like a *Sports Illustrated* swimsuit issue come to life. He mentioned that his buddy even knew my boyhood hero, current Dodgers manager Don Mattingly, and claimed we would get to meet him. My eyes and ears perked up. WOW. A chance to meet "Donnie Baseball"? I was in. As exciting and amazing as this midday baseball excursion sounded, I hesitantly asked Ray the necessary question.

"Can I bring my son with us?"

Ray ordered two more beers.

"You don't listen, do you?" he said.

Looking up at the spring training baseball game on the TV, I thought back to all the days I had spent in the sun collecting autographs and anxiously awaiting handshakes and smiles from my big league heroes growing up in Tucson. I remembered trying to get my dad to take me to as many games as possible, and his typical fatherly response:

"Sometimes the best seat is on your own couch," he would say.

That quote always made me angry. To me the best seat was *anywhere inside the ballpark*, where a kid could take in the sights and sounds of the game while eating sodium-stuffed foods with mustard and relish smothered all over his jeans. However, it took me a long time to figure out how much work it actually is to get yourself motivated to get out and attend a baseball game in person, especially when you are taking your kids. Still, when Ray promised me opening day Dodgers tickets, I knew I would have to figure out a way to get my son in with me. Without him, the game was just another afternoon drinking beer with Ray.

The rest of the afternoon devolved into a drunken blur. Ray bought round after round as we hopped from one bar in the Hollywood area to another. I texted my wife that I was out "helping Ray get his shit together" when in reality, I was hoisting pints of Pabst Blue Ribbon in the air at 3:30 on a Tuesday afternoon, laughing with my old college buddy while screaming, "Guess I'm not making that spinning class, am I?"

We flirted with waitresses, played video poker, ate chicken wings and onion rings and terrible mini-meatballs, played the jukebox, and watched hours of college basketball at a Cahuenga joint called "Big Wangs". We rifled through memories of college and girls and drugs and drinking and music and my GOD it was as stress-free and perfect as any married father of two inching his way towards 40 could feel.

In fact, it felt like I was 21 again.

"Stay as long as you like," I yelled again at Ray.

Little did I know, I would be sharing my living room couch with Ray that evening.

My wife was waiting for us as we stumbled through the door a few hours later, angry that I had blown off the entire day to get drunk with Ray. Apparently, I had missed my son's Tae Kwon Do practice and forgotten to make dinner for the kids. I tossed a leftover container of limp French fries on the counter, mentioning that they were really tasty. My wife just rolled her eyes. As she trudged upstairs to bed, Ray and I were laughing and hugging like we were back at Pacific Beach on his wedding day. Only difference was, I wasn't passed out in the sand, and his wife was nowhere to be seen.

That night, my wife told me to sleep on the couch.

Citing that Ray was already there, she said she didn't care; she tossed me into the living room with only a pillow and a thin blanket to keep warm. Drearily, I crept along the floor until I found a warmish place to lay my head and did my best to crash out. In my buzzed state, I forgot that Ray was on the couch and I climbed into the sofa next to him. He promptly nudged me back onto the faux-sheepskin rug. Oddly enough, from then on I slept like a prince in a royal bed. Maybe it was because my kids weren't jumping on me at six in the morning, but I felt like a well-rested Olympic champion the next day when I woke up on my living room floor on a grilled cheese-stained rug that, for a few hours, felt like a miniscule slice of restful heaven.

My wife startled me the next day by announcing she was off to the gym again. Feeling somewhat tousled and incapable of a four-mile treadmill jog, I decided that I would help Ray get his stuff together before setting out to find him a new place to live. I was being a good friend to a guy who had once been a good friend to me. It was as if all the time we spent together in college was now being cashed in, and I was an investor willing to pay back my corporation tenfold.

I soon found out that Ray had no intention of ever leaving.

After viewing about six apartments (all of which were either "too small", "too big" or "had a strange smell"), we rolled into a Johnny Rockets hamburger stand on Melrose Avenue, a place I frequented back when I had a metabolism but at the current time avoided at all costs. Following Ray's lead, we ordered French fries and vinegar and sat watching the cute girls and flamboyant EDM freaks travel down the boulevard looking to shock the *Rolling Stone* folks during the following month out at Coachella.

As I longed for my youth, when the girls dressed like Lady Miss Kier and the men wore Motorola pagers tucked inside their waistbands, I considered my options in my head as I watched Ray drizzle ketchup on his hamburger. There was work piling up at home that I had blown off, but there was also no rush to get anything done. Ray wasn't exactly upset with his current situation, but he was certainly aware that this little honeymoon phase of being single and acting like a cad would soon be coming to a close. He reminded me of Alan Wieder in his overlooked but frighteningly real novel *Year of the Cock*. Ray was scoping young girls, checking surf reports on his phone, and preparing to start drinking again once the clock struck five. Of course, I would be expected to join him.

I was back on the sheepskin rug that night.

And the next.

With one day to go before we were to attend opening day, my wife was barely talking to me. That morning, as we nursed our throbbing hangovers, my three-year-old daughter decided to play her mini toy drum kit at six in the morning. The kit was a gift from my father and stepmother, following an iPhone video we shot of our little girl drumming on two books with a set of Olive Garden breadsticks. My dad, an amateur drummer himself, saw in my daughter the next Ringo Starr, and for her birthday, a new drum set arrived into our lives. Ever since then she had largely ignored the drum kit, but had decided that today, the night after an avalanche of Irish Car Bombs at The Pikey on Sunset, she was Keith fucking Moon.

Clang clang clang, crash clang boom clang clang. The ringing was unbearable. Beneath my blanket I was cursing my father for this gift. Why couldn't he have sprung for a LaLa Loopsy Doll? Bastard. As Ray and I covered our heads with pillows, attempting to drown out the literal pounding everywhere, I swear I heard my wife snickering as if to say, "Go ahead baby, wake up these two bums and show them that real life doesn't work when you drink until three in the morning and still expect to be a good father."

More clanging. More crashing. More pain.

Finally, Ray stood up and grabbed the drumsticks from my daughter. He had stopped the hellish cacophony of toddler drumming, but he had also unleashed a fury that went unmatched in the world of upset three-year-olds.

Oh, the screaming.

As my wife snatched back the drumsticks, she scoffed at Ray's inconsiderate and assumptive move to take her sticks away. He had ceased to exist as another roommate; he had become the *enemy*. A drifter on the couch. A liquored-up vision of what MY life would become if I continued to let this guy hang out for even one hour longer.

"Zach, get in here," my wife yelled. "Either he leaves, or you leave."

Well, the writing was on the wall. I had partied it up long enough with Ray to find the strength to tell him that he needed to get off the couch and move into a one bedroom apartment in Koreatown or elsewhere. It was time he left. I invited him down the street for lunch as a way to lower the boom in a public place so that he wouldn't break a window or smash a beer bottle in my home. We went back to Birds.

I was supposed to break it on down: tell him that he had overstayed his welcome and become a burden on our house, that his lifestyle was beginning to not only affect my marriage, but our friendship as well. I was supposed to shoulder the blame and fire reason after reason why he could no longer squat on our living room couch clutching a beer and the remote control. It was *my* responsibility.

Instead, I blamed it all on my wife.

Surprisingly, Ray seemed to take it very well. He did not mention that I had told him a month would be fine merely five days prior. He did not mention that he had saved my life on his wedding night all those years ago. Nor did he mention that he had been buying beer and food for the house like any decent unwelcome houseguest would do in a time of reliance on a friend for shelter.

Instead, he bought another round and said, "Guess you won't be coming to opening day then, huh?"

I'm not sure if this was an attempt at a guilt trip to send me reeling back home to beg my wife for another week, but it certainly made me realize that Ray was a man who truly didn't care much about the dilemmas of fatherhood. After all, had I gone to opening day with Ray, and not my baseball-obsessed son, my wife would have killed me. It's something that fathers *do with their sons.* Responsible dads don't send their kid to the playground so they can go drink 12 dollar Bud Lights with a bunch of XVIII Street gang members shouting hellacious things at a field of grass and dirt. Responsible dads don't sleep on the floor of their living room for three nights in a row. Responsible dads certainly do not drink beer at 12:30 on a Friday afternoon just to get through the rest of the daylight hours. I had to tell Ray it was time to go.

"If that's what your wife wants, I guess it's cool," he said. "Wow, kicked out by two wives in the same week. Bummer."

So this morning, Ray thanked my wife and my kids for the hospitality and limped out of our front door towards his motorcycle. He was Dodgers opening day bound, along with some friends and a girl he had invited from Facebook who had worked for him as a pinstriper when he was designing surfboards. We waved to each other and nodded as if to say, *See you down the road.*

As he rode off, I reached down and rubbed my son's head as he looked up at me with oddly curious eyes.

"So, we're not going to the baseball game today, dad?" he asked.

A smile ran across my face as I tossed a wiffle ball into his new Mizuno left-handed mitt. I smiled at my wife and daughter, who seemed relieved that Ray had finally gone his merry way. I thought about how upset I was to not be meeting Don Mattingly, and how much a hot dog and a beer on opening day makes all the world's troubles disappear. Then I looked down at my son and said these words, understanding their meaning for the first time:

"You know, sometimes the best seat is on your own couch."

Father of the Year

Based on my calculations, I have probably nursed more than 3,500 hangovers in my adult life. Most of them have been passable, usually unraveling before 10 a.m. with some coffee, greasy food, and copious amounts of water. Others have traveled into the afternoon, resisting all the old tricks: boxes of coconut water, bottles of Kombucha, and the occasional trip to the steam room.

Then there are those hangovers that creep into the next day. Those hangovers that have you seriously considering a treatment program or moving out to a deserted island far away from the temptations of the real world; a place where you can dry out and kick the need to drink every time your favorite team scores a run, you watch a film like *Pulp Fiction*, or read a rock-n-roll autobiography.

As I have grown older, those two-to-three day hangovers happen a lot less frequently; I can barely recall the last time I had a mind-crusher that took me out for an entire day. However, on October 27, 2012, at 5:42 in the morning, my two-and-a-half-year-old daughter woke me up by screaming to the largest mule-kick, thunder-fuck of a hangover I have ever had in my 37 years on planet Earth.

It was one of those "I'd rather just die here" hangovers. A "I'm considering just vomiting in my bed" hangover. My brain shrieked in anguish as I attempted to focus on any inanimate object in my bedroom. I was as useful as a deflated pool raft, a moppish blob of failure.

It was at that moment that I remembered it was Saturday morning, and I was expected to fulfill a laundry list of activities throughout the day, activities I had no memory of agreeing to but were saved in my iPhone calendar.

At 10 am, my family was scheduled to meet another family at the Los Angeles Zoo for a Halloween-themed afternoon where there was supposed to be all types of fun activities, free candy, and spooky decorations; the event was called *Boo at the Zoo*, and my wife had planned it a week earlier. Unfortunately, my wife had also forgotten that she had to work all day Saturday, so I would be hanging with both kids by myself.

Then, at 3 o'clock, we had a one-year-old's birthday party at a park in Sherman Oaks to go to.

It should be noted that my six-year-old son had broken his foot a week earlier by jumping off a jungle gym and was sporting a massive cast, so I was dreading any activity that would take place outdoors and make him feel useless. Unfortunately, both of these plans were outdoor events.

To top it all off, I checked the weather forecast for the day: a hellish 90-plus degrees in late October.

Fuck me.

The piercing screech of my daughter demanding a bowl of Cheerios was a fierce reminder that I am no longer able to drink like I used to. I could barely walk as I carried her downstairs into the living room, where I promptly did what any terrific, hands-on parent who cares about his children's future would do…

I turned on the TV and crawled beneath a blanket.

Despite the din of *Mickey Mouse Clubhouse*, I was able to quickly rediscover my sleep pattern; I drifted in and out of consciousness as Mickey and Goofy talked about calling some freak named "Toodles" for help with their project. I figured I was good to go. The blanket was a little thin, but the couch never felt better. I was convinced I could skate by another two hours and be in fine shape to take the little ones to *Boo at the Zoo*. It was then my six-year-old son woke up.

"Are we going to the zoo yet, daddy?" he asked.

"Uhghghg… I think the zoo is closed today…" I said.

"No, Mommy said it was open. Can I have Frosted Flakes?"

When my wife woke up, she was ebullient over the fact that she was to spend the day interviewing orphans for a documentary film she was producing. I know her project is important, but I insensitively insulted the entire thing from beneath my shield of a blanket anyway.

"I'm real glad you care more about the orphans than you do your own kids," I remarked.

And with that, she was out the door for her interviews, obviously pissed off at me not only for my immature comment, but also for my gargantuan hangover.

As I pulled myself into an upright state, I tried to piece together my activity from the night before and remember exactly where it all went wrong, at what moment the tables had turned and I had blacked out. For some reason, I was running a lot of blank tape. And then it hit me…it was my trainer Tony's fault!

Tony and I had met at the gym a year earlier. He was solely responsible for transforming my body from a doughy, out-of-shape 36-year-old into the only slightly less doughy, out-of-shape 37-year-old writing this essay. (Truth be told, Tony has helped me shed ten pounds and get into my best shape since high school…but that's another story.) Tony is a beast. At the gym he throws me into gravity strength training classes, punishing me with his signature moves called "Burpees", "Oil-wells", and "Gorilla Thumps". I leave the gym in pain every time we work out together, but I have seen incredible results; I look at the guy not only as a trainer, but as a new friend. However, up until the night before, we had never been out drinking together.

Tony had texted me that he wanted to have a beer somewhere in Hollywood. Feeling a little loopy following the bottle of wine my wife and I had split during bath time with our kids, I was intrigued to go and join a healthy athlete like Tony on a pub crawl. My wife told me to have fun, and specifically warned me not to drink too much.

"Please," I said. "He's a trainer. I highly doubt he likes to drink excessively."

Oh, how wrong I was.

Apparently, Tony has the same sort of mentality towards drinking in a bar as he does in a weight room or a gravity class. He is a leader. The kind of guy who pushes you to do the things that don't make you feel good. So, as forcefully as he made me do twenty pull-ups in the gym, he got me to do nine shots at the bar. It was the trainer mentality that said, "Do it, or you're a pussy."

So, I did it. And I did it a lot. Convinced I could easily dust him in any kind of drinking contest, I was shocked when he continued blasting through shots of Jameson as I casually switched over to light beer. His constant ribbing of my "weak liver" only fueled me to turn back to doing shots, and by the time midnight rolled around I was so hammered I was bumming menthol cigarettes from a prostitute named "Mouse".

The last thing I remember was having a final glass of red wine at the bar down the street from my house before walking home to my awaiting bedroom, where I promptly knocked over a shelf full of books, barely making it under the sheets. I slept in my contact lenses. My wife said my breathing was so beleaguered that she feared I might asphyxiate during the night. To top it all off, I tried to listen to music on my iPhone as I went to sleep, but instead ended up dropping it and extending a small crack in the face of the phone all the way down across the home button. The next thing I knew, 5:42 am arrived and I was carrying the little girl downstairs.

After my wife left, I attempted another tried-and-true father maneuver to divert my children from wanting to go to the *Boo at the Zoo* celebration; I bribed them.

"Listen," I said to the boy. "If we skip the zoo today, I'll buy you any Skylanders toy you want. Either that, or I'll take you to get ice-cream sundaes later."

"Can't we have both?" he asked.

I rubbed a moon rock of sleep from my eye.

"Sure," I relented.

Roughly thirty minutes later, the cereal was all over the floor and the kids were fighting over what channel they wanted to watch. Feeling somewhat guilty, I informed them that we were not going to watch any more TV and that we were going to the park.

"But what about the zoo?" the boy yelled.

Raising children is not an easy thing. Especially when you are an aging almost-rock star who once released an album called "Alcoholiday". You get used to the night life for so long, it is a 180 degree wake-up call the first time your kid jolts you up in the early morning ruining what was once uninterrupted sleep. I am not the first person to write about this type of stuff, but I may be one of the first to try and do what I used to whenever things didn't go my way in life: drink through it.

I managed to put together the most comfortable outfit I could, comprised of a dirty sweatshirt off the floor, cargo shorts, and flip flops. I loaded up a bag full of kids' snacks and bottles for the zoo. Ten was quickly approaching and I thought that perhaps, with a little more water and a Power Bar, I could get through the twenty minute drive to the zoo for what was sure to be a fun day for my kids. After all, my wife would absolutely kill me if I kept them at home to nurse a hangover, so I sacked up and decided that a little fresh air might do us all some good. (By the way, if you are wondering why I have yet to pop an Advil or Tylenol, it's because I am afraid of pain-relief medicine. Yeah, I know. I will take nine shots of Jameson, but I am afraid of the physical damage two Advil might do to my body. I admit it. I am a flawed man.)

I should have turned the car around when I saw the traffic entering Griffith Park. We were backed up for 25 minutes. The number of cars going left seemed endless, and I immediately knew that the zoo would be a madhouse. Still, I turned up the volume on the backseat TV and let the kids watch the final half hour of *Monsters vs. Aliens*. I also took the time to begin texting the other family we were going to meet at the zoo. Scott and Joely weren't close friends, but they had a six-year-old who my son enjoyed playing with. Besides I thought, another two sets of eyes would make the day go by a lot faster.

I texted Scott.

How close are you guys?

He didn't reply.

After we successfully made the left turn into Griffith Park, we followed the winding road around past the golf course and up towards the Gene Autry Museum and the Los Angeles Zoo. I slouched forward and noticed the alarming number of cars already parked in the adjacent lot. Families of four pushed strollers towards the entrance roughly 2,000 feet away from the nearest parking space. I should have turned around. Instead, I passed through the barricade and committed to the afternoon. I looked at my phone; 88 degrees and rising.

My headache only worsened as I wrestled the stroller from the back of my car. Sometimes, trying to maneuver a stroller into position is like attempting to fold a 30-pound origami napkin. Wheels get turned sideways, diaper bags get caught in bottom carriages…it truly sucks. Of course on this day of hangover hell, everything you can imagine was going wrong. When I finally straightened it out and prepared for the half-mile hike to the entrance, I carried my daughter towards the stroller, praying she'd take a nap for the majority of the zoo adventure. Instead, she wanted to walk. The boy, already lame in his foot cast, wanted to go in the stroller. Realizing that it would probably be a better idea for him to not put as much pressure on his foot, I let him ride. Of course, this made the girl want to ride as well.

The brother-sister battle began. As I strained to push the stroller with a 55-pound boy inside, my daughter screamed that now she wanted to ride. I compromised by carrying her in my left arm while pushing the boy with my right. We made it roughly 25 feet before I had to readjust and try another tactic. If she couldn't go in the stroller, her only other desire was to be carried. It was finalized; I would be carrying my daughter the entire time we were at the zoo.

Just at we arrived at the entrance, Scott finally texted me back.

Dude, waaaay too crowded and hot. We're not gonna make it. Beer later?

Fuck you, Scott.

Boo at the Zoo was one of the lamest things you could choose to take your children to. In the newspaper ad, kids were promised trick-or-treating and huge bags of candy. Upon arrival, they were handed a tiny paper bag with five treats inside, sponsored by 99 Cent stores. The giant pumpkin maze turned out to be seven bales of hay arranged in a small stack surrounded by random jack-o'-lanterns. The "spooky crafts" they had been promised was a table where you could paint a stick. Finally, there was an attraction where zookeepers fed chimpanzees pumpkins and let the crowd watch.

At one point, while leaning over the tapir cage, a father standing next to me sniffed near my body and made eye contact.

"Dude, I didn't want to say anything, but you smell like booze," he said.

I slowly turned my head towards the sober-looking instigator.

"Walk away," I growled.

The boy seemed to get heavier as the day wore on, possibly because I let him eat his entire treat bag; he simply refused to get out of the stroller. The girl and I actually saw most of the animals, which was somewhat enjoyable, especially when she called the giraffe a "firaffe" and the zebra a "webra". But mainly, it was just another day at the zoo with a ferocious hangover and 2,000 families in Halloween costumes jockeying for position to watch a Brazilian rodent called a "red-rumped agouti" eat pumpkin seeds.

Having nursed mild hangovers everywhere from Disneyland to farmer's markets, I have to say the LA Zoo has one terrific advantage: it serves booze. At first I didn't notice, but as the day dragged on I saw more and more parents were nursing twelve dollar beers in the now 91-degree heat. I even saw a kiosk offering up red and white wine and toyed with the idea of a little "hair of the dog", but my stomach pains eventually won out and I continued to swallow water at a feverish pace instead. About two hours into our zoo journey, I broke a natural sweat. It felt terrific. I let the girl run around near the elephant display as I soaked up the sun like a *Jersey Shore* cast member in a tanning booth. I finally felt, for the first time all day, alive.

I bought the kids some chips and a hot dog to split, but neither of them seemed interested. Frustrated by the fact that I had just dropped $15 on a hot dog and bag of Doritos, I decided that I would be eating them myself. I wheeled the stroller to the edge of the "Gorilla Grill" and proceeded to wolf down the nitrate-blasted chemical dog and chips, and even went back inside to order a chocolate-dipped churro. The boy sulked when I wouldn't let him have any of the churro; I told him he needed to eat something healthy before he could have a treat. This coming from a guy who just poisoned his body with thirty gallons of liquor and a frankfurter made out of pig lips, intestines, and assholes.

After I washed down the food with a soda, some color returned to my face and I felt less peaked. I wheeled the stroller around the lion display (closed) and past another Halloween activity (the pumpkin-carving specialist) before announcing that this day at the zoo was over.

I steadied myself for the mile-and-a-half walk back to the car. All I cared about was getting home, putting the girl down for her nap, and watching any college football game on TV. I could blame her nap schedule for us missing the one-year-old's birthday (everyone does it); I just knew that if I didn't lie down soon, things might get really ugly. My wife wasn't due home until 7:30, so I figured that some coffee and TV might help me drift through the rest of the day. I limped off towards our ride home.

Thirty minutes later, I battled with the stroller again and climbed into the wretchedly hot interior of my wife's 2002 Honda CR-V.

I sat and let the air conditioning pulsate through the car. The boy looked miserable, jamming a pretzel stick into his leg cast to scratch an invisible itch.

Of course, the pretzel broke off, and I spent the next fourteen minutes trying to dig it out. My daughter repeatedly asked for a bottle, throwing the half-water concoction I tried to pass off as milk back at me in the front seat.

I pulled out of the parking lot and turned the wheel towards home. I knew the day was only half over, but the worst part of my hangover had passed… or so I thought. My head was still pounding and now, following my disgusting lunch, my stomach had kicked itself into high gear as well. As it rumbled through the drive home, I thought about texting Scott back and cursing him out for skipping the zoo altogether. At this point, I had two choices: I could tell Scott how lucky he was that he had skipped it, and give him the sense of satisfaction that he had made the right decision to stay home instead; or I could talk up the experience as one of the best we as a family had ever been a part of. I went with the latter.

Boo at the Zoo RULED! Best day ever – we missed you guys… it was amazing and not too hot!

Evil, I know, but it made me feel a little better.

Five minutes from the house, I nearly puked in my car. I realized that it was probably going to happen within the next thirty minutes, so I did my best to hold it in as we rambled down Franklin Avenue. As I fought back the acidic demons in my stomach, I looked back at my kids and hoped that they had had at least a morsel of fun. I know the boy was too injured to do much, but he at least got to see a few neat things, and for that I felt proud of myself as a dad. I had braved the crowds, the heat, and the zoo and even had a little laugh about the entire experience. I asked my daughter what her favorite part was, and she responded with, "The firaffe." My heart nearly melted.

I then asked my son. Keenly aware that he had just been wheeled around a 91-degree zoo with a broken foot, he tossed back something that only a six-year-old could hold onto after nearly half a day spent surrounded by strange families in costumes eating bags of treats from a 99 cent store…

He scratched at his cast and the bits of pretzel stick still hanging around the itchy part of his poor leg and caught my eye in the rear-view mirror. He squinted his eyes back at me before responding…

"Dad?" he said. "When are going to get ice cream sundaes?"

Honeysuckle

There is a small stretch of road about five minutes from my house that is known as "Tranny Alley", which exists on what used to be the most famous highway in America: Route 66. Nowadays, it is known simply as Santa Monica Boulevard, running the length of the city and cascading into the Pacific Ocean at its conclusion.

"Tranny Alley" gets its name from, you guessed it, the number of transsexual prostitutes working their trade up and down the boulevard. Situated directly between Highland Avenue and Las Palmas Boulevard, the majority of these prostitutes seem to use a shop called "Donut Time" as their home base. It was there that I found myself picking up a 28-year-old prostitute named "Honeysuckle".

Any man who has lived in the City of Angels for any period of time has at some point found himself staring at a tight pair of denim shorts walking down the street only to be surprised when the person turns around and reveals him/herself as a guy. Santa Monica Boulevard is usually the place where it all goes down. Sometimes, they catch you staring and send an awkward wink your way, at which point you react by either looking the other way or thinking to yourself, *Wow… Dude or not, I still got it!*

Last week, when I was on my way to pick up my six-year-old son from school, I noticed a pair of those exact denim shorts parading across a parking lot in the heart of Tranny Alley. Sensing my gaze, she sent a flirtatious look my way as I watched her slink towards Donut Time. She was by far the prettiest girl I have ever seen in Tranny Alley in the 19 years I have lived in this city; there was even something familiar about her I couldn't quite place. She had a body like Rihanna and a face like a young Sage Steele. If she was in fact a man, she was so gorgeous I didn't care.

As I scooped up my six-year-old from school and we began driving home, I decided to take Santa Monica Boulevard again, risking a Donut Time drive-by. My son never fails to notice whenever we pass a shop serving up the fried, round, sugary treats. He has a Jedi-like ability to him and can sense a donut shop whenever we are within 15 feet of one. It's amazing. Now giving your kid a donut at 3:30 in the afternoon is a terrible idea, as it often leads to a sugar crash, Lego's being thrown all around your house, and a dinner time screaming match between my wife and I. However, the moment I passed the shop, I noticed Rihanna again, and she noticed me as well. She gave me a subtle nod and winked, just as my son yelled out at the top of his lungs,

"Donuts!"

I flipped on my blinker and made a left turn into the parking lot.

I did not intend to speak to her. I just wanted to get inside the shop, pick out a donut, maybe get a closer look at Rihanna, and then speed off towards the park to make my son run off the 550 calories he had just inhaled. Instead, she approached me like a long lost girlfriend just as I walked through the door.

"You go to the Hollywood YMCA, don't you?" she asked as I cradled my son so he could get a better look into the donut case.

How the hell did she know that?

"Uhhm, yeah?" I said quizzically. "Are you a… member?"

She laughed. I glanced at her throat. It was Adam's apple free.

"I shower there sometimes," she continued. "I've seen you and your kid walking around."

It was then that I put it together. She *was* a member of the Hollywood YMCA. I had seen her before, striding around the ground floor, making every pasty-white mother of three uncomfortable by flaunting her ferocious curves and Olympian build. I had always assumed she was a personal trainer or a professional fitness model or something; looks like she was simply, a professional.

"Are you a…" I started, before looking down at my son, knowing that no six-year-old should be conversing with a prostitute ten minutes after leaving Math Workshop.

She smiled and rubbed the side of my shoulder.

"I can be anything you want me to be."

Now I have never been one for talking dirty, but for some reason, her comment uncoiled some inner beast in my loins that had been lying dormant for way too long. I noticed a boulder-like erection burst forth in my boxer briefs. This girl's voice and body and face were so searing, for one fleeting moment I truly considered throwing away a perfect marriage to the love of my life and consenting to spend the rest of my adulthood couch-surfing in Van Nuys. I felt at peace with the fact that I would rarely be allowed to see my children again. And if my wife wanted to take half of my finances? FINE. These all seemed like worthy sacrifices for one night of rapture with a thunder-bodied sex bomb who looked like she could break my penis off.

And who may or may not be a guy.

I paid for the donut and did my best to shake off the fantasy. As I willed my erection to lower itself to half mast, I eeked a smile her way and raised my hand, showing her my wedding ring as if to say, "Sorry, I'm married."

She laughed and whispered into my ear.

"Single men don't walk into Donut Time," she said. "Most of my regulars are married...but you're the first guy who actually brought his kid along."

I looked over at the boy eating his chocolate sprinkled donut, unaware that his father could be twenty minutes away from making the biggest mistake of his life. Unaware that we were in "Tranny Alley", thinking only of ninjas and the Angry Birds *Star Wars* toy on his Hannukkah list. Innocent, pure and happy.

"It's fifty bucks for a blow-job," she whispered.

"We should go," I yelled out to the boy. "C'mon, dude..."

I loaded him up into the car and didn't even buckle his seat belt. His face was smeared with chocolate. Within minutes, we were at the park; he climbed a play structure while I perversely Googled "sexy Rihanna images" on my iPhone. Had anybody seen some of the half-naked images I came across, I would have been arrested and thrown in prison for lewd conduct; looking at soft-core porn on your phone in a public park felt like a bigger offense than actually picking up a prostitute. (I looked that up by the way... It's not.)

Paranoid, I cleared my history, turned off my phone, and did ten pull-ups on the monkey bars as a way to release some unbridled energy.

I realized that I didn't have my wallet about 45 minutes later. We had come home from the park and the Rihanna incident was way behind me, erased by other concerns: what time was his soccer practice? Did I forget to email the bank about the house Re-Fi? Why did I forget to buy printer ink? But all of these questions were cast aside by the horrifying realization that my wallet was gone, and the only place it could possibly be was sitting on the counter at Donut Time.

When my wife came home, I told her I had left my wallet at my son's school and I had to go get it. She called me a dumb-ass and told me to hurry up, we had Nick and Marcy coming over for dinner. I jumped in the car and raced towards Santa Monica Boulevard as fast as I could, praying that Rihanna was nowhere to be found and that my wallet was safe and sound behind the counter. I was mortified, as nervous as a high school kid on a first date.

As I began creeping down Tranny Alley, I noticed that there were a few more "ladies" of the night walking the street. I managed to find a parking spot at a meter, hoping my presence would go unnoticed. I crossed over the sidewalk and ran towards Donut Time at a swift pace. As I opened the door, a familiar voice turned me around.

"Looking for this?"

There was Rihanna, holding my embarrassing tri-panel Velcro piece of shit wallet with a clear sleeve for my driver's license and a change purse zipper. My driver's license was in her left hand.

"Zachary Stephen Selwyn, huh?" she said. "You look younger than 37."

"Uhm, thanks," I said, not knowing if she really meant it or if it was her way to talk a potential john into dropping 500 bucks on life-ruining sex.

"Where'd you, uhh – find it?" I asked.

"I can find a man's wallet anywhere. Now you want it back, or what?"

"Yes please," I meekly answered.

"You can have it…if you run me up to the YMCA. I have to take a shower."

The first thing that popped into my mind was the Hugh Grant/Divine Brown incident. Back in 1997, Grant was arrested for receiving fellatio in his BMW just north of Tranny Alley from a prostitute named Divine Brown. Following the arrest, Grant's reputation went from "irresistibly charming leading man" to 'Mickey Blue Eyes.' Divine Brown, meanwhile, has allegedly made close to two million dollars from personal appearances and pornography and is now raising her three well-off children in Beverly Hills. Advantage: Prostitute.

Around the same time, Eddie Murphy was pulled over with a tranny prostitute in his car in the same neighborhood. Although never charged with anything, Eddie was dragged across the floor by the press. By offering Rihanna a ride, I was risking my career and more importantly, my marriage. It seemed like a no-win situation.

"Sure, I can give you a ride," I said.

I wasn't sure why I had agreed to do it. It was a moment of weakness, where I felt like "Mr. Incredible" from *The Incredibles*. Downtrodden, bored, and eager to find adventure again, he takes on paid missions without his wife to get his mojo back. Of course he ends up nearly dying, until his superhero family arrives and saves his ass and they all live happily ever after. I wondered to myself if my superhero family would come save me should I get arrested with a prostitute in the front seat of my car…

Probably not.

Rihanna handed me my wallet and tried to hold my hand as we walked back to my car. I pushed it away and kept my eyes peeled for any sign of police. For the moment, everything looked clear. We got in and I quickly lowered the volume on my radio so she wouldn't know I had been playing Rihanna's "What's my Name" on my iPod for the past thirty minutes. We pulled out into traffic and headed towards Vine, where the lucky YMCA showers would see her naked instead of me.

"OK, you know my name…what's yours?" I asked her. After all, I couldn't keep referring to her as "Rihanna".

She took a moment to fiddle around with a pair of sunglasses I had resting against the center console. She put them on and turned towards me.

"You can call me Honeysuckle," she said.

Could there be a more appropriate name for this fiery African-American fuck machine than "Honeysuckle"? It was perfect.

"Is that your real name?" I asked.

"Is Zachary your real name?"

"Uhh, yeah."

"Then my real name is Honeysuckle."

"Wow!" I said. "Like the Willie Nelson film *Honeysuckle Rose*!"

"Never seen it."

As she lowered the passenger side mirror to apply lipstick, I found it odd that she was on her way to take a shower and was applying make-up ten minutes beforehand. She pursed her lips and laughed at her face in the mirror, exuding more self-confidence than any woman I feel I had ever encountered. It was the last thing you expected a "soiled dove" to be doing. I dug deeper, fascinated by this workhorse of sexual pleasure. I have always been obsessed with those who spend their lives this way; I love their back-stories and their ideals, and hearing about the unique way they view the world. Her story was enthralling.

As it turned out, Honeysuckle was born and raised in Oakland by a single mother who was also a prostitute. She dropped out of high school at 16 when she got pregnant, then lost the baby during childbirth. Disenchanted with everything, she moved to San Francisco were she began turning tricks for as much as $1,500 a night. By 21 she was well-known throughout the city, pleasuring star athletes, politicians and businessmen from all over the world. She had even once been flown to New York for a convention with top brass at a massive electronics company we all know. Finally she settled in LA, where she heard she might be able to work as a high-class call girl and not a "streetwalker". Unfortunately, most of the girls in Los Angeles in that racket were five to ten years younger and from foreign countries. Honeysuckle claimed she was too street savvy to get caught up in what she called "Ho Business" and she now walks the boulevard three times a week, doing what she can to keep her lights turned on, her weave silky, and her body in shape. It was a story straight out of a terrible movie. A hooker with a heart of gold? I wasn't sure what I believed.

I had one more question I had to ask her. I took a chance.

"So, by any chance… are you a transsexual?" I boldly proposed.

"Honey, please – I am all woman," she exclaimed. "You know what my father once told me before he split on me and my mom? He gave me the best piece of advice I have ever heard: *As long as you got a pussy, you will never go broke.*"

I took that in. I have absolutely no plans of ever sharing that advice with my two-and-a-half-year-old daughter.

We drove in silence for a few blocks as she applied more makeup and drank from a mini bottle of grape Five-Hour Energy tucked away in her purse. I was only hoping to make it to the destination without seeing any flashing red and blue lights in my rearview mirror. As we made a left onto Selma near the new Trader Joe's, I finally broke the silence.

"So, why do you belong to the YMCA?" I asked.

"The Y lets homeless people in on a ten-dollar-a-month discounted rate," she explained. "I'd say 50-100 YMCA members are homeless people or hookers…it's true. Trust me, do NOT go in the Jacuzzi."

I had taken my six-year-old boy in the Jacuzzi two days earlier.

As we pulled up to the front of the YMCA, it suddenly dawned on me that I had seen a number of toothless men in the locker rooms, shady looking women emerging from the massage rooms and occasional clove-smoking dope fiends shuffling in and out of the front door. Maybe Honeysuckle was telling the truth; the Hollywood Y was as much a gym, a gravity strength pilates class, and a Kids Klub, as it was a homeless shelter. I was about to cut my engine when Honeysuckle instructed me to pull to the side of the building.

I did as I was told, the rhino horn of a boner I had sported earlier now completely retreated inside of my body. I pulled my car into a metered space and watched her smooth out her shorts so they wouldn't bunch up. She casually stared back at me and put her hand on my upper thigh.

"The best thing about a woman like me, Zachary, is that I don't kiss and tell," she said.

I looked deep into her hazel eyes. She was a marvelous physical specimen, probably no older than 27 or 28. Any man with the money to spend was sure to have the time of his life with this woman; but I was simply not going to be that guy. All I could think of was my son and the chocolate smeared across his face and his Hannukkah list and my wife's smile and my daughter's growing Hello Kitty collection. I was even looking forward to the small argument about getting the boy a donut at 3:30 in the afternoon.

I just wanted to go home.

Honeysuckle kept her hand on my thigh. I thought long and hard about how I was gong to let her down without crushing her. I mean, her life had been so hard, could she handle my rejection? How would she react? I was nervous. I took a deep breath and reached down into the depths of my soul for what was the honest-to-God truth.

"Look, I'm flattered…but I – I can't – I could never live with myself," I said.

Without flinching, her hand was gone from my leg. She clicked her tongue against the roof of her mouth and opened the door. Within eight seconds, she had left my car, tossed her weave back over her shoulders, and buckled her purse. So much for her having trouble taking rejection.

As she walked away from my car towards the YMCA, I found myself watching her denim shorts again. It was then that she turned around and ran back to my window. *I knew it*, I thought. She had to know how this 37-year-old father and husband could have turned down her advances…

As she persuaded me to roll down my window, I expected another come-on. *After all these years, I still got it,* I reassured myself. After all, getting hit on by any woman at my age is flattering, even if they turn out to be a prostitute. I zapped down the pane and awaited her final cry for my love.

"Hey, Zachary," she began. "You had fifty bucks in your wallet when I found it, so I took it as a finder's fee, okay?"

***

I've driven by Tranny Alley a few times since, but Honeysuckle seems to have disappeared. I hadn't seen her at the YMCA either, until earlier this week. I caught her bounding out of the locker room, midriff showing, with micro-beads of sweat glistening just above her belly button. As usual, all the YMCA moms stopped and stared, and the older dudes working out on the machines snuck glances as she sauntered towards the door. As she passed by my wife and I, she caught my eye and gave me a small nod. I smiled back, feeling happy knowing that she was still around, and had no intention of changing who she was to appease others.

"Wow," my wife said. "I think that hot black chick just checked you out!"

I jokingly flexed my bicep in her face and sucked in my cheeks like some duck-mouthed supermodel.

"Still got it," I said.

Four Old Guys Go To A Phish Show (Phish Story)

In 1995, I had hair down to my back, owned 329 bootleg Phish cassette tapes and dated a girl who didn't shave her armpits, with whom I shared a cat named "Fee". Phish was more than a band to me; they were a way of life. Whenever they happened within 300 miles of Los Angeles, I was out the door and into the Honda Civic I had named "Hayley's Comet" (after one of their songs) en route to another show somewhere down the road. In the 19 years since my first concert, I have seen Phish in 13 different states (and many altered ones). I have snuck into their dressing rooms during long jam sets and taken pictures of their guitar cases. I even went to Europe in 1996 to follow them around as they opened – yes, opened - for Santana. The highlights of this trip included meeting Trey Anastasio in an Amsterdam café and shaking Mike Gordon's hand outside of the venue in Paris, as well as making out with plenty of European women.

Yes, I was fanatical. Phish was even the reason I decided to "join the internet", just to check out their website Phish.net. They were the benchmark of a person's character. Did you like Phish? *No?* Sorry, we can't be friends.

Every one of my close friends was right there with me. We would send letters with set lists from East Coast shows to buddies stuck in LA along with tapes, make mixes, and throw listening parties. Throughout the years, some of us had been cited for possession, arrested for selling bootleg t-shirts, and handcuffed at DUI checkpoints. On a dare, my friend Frisco Freddy got married while on ecstasy to a girl he met at the Aladdin Theatre in Las Vegas at a drive-through chapel following the show. They danced to "If I Could" and made love in a hotel room shared by twelve people that night; we all giggled listening to Frisco Freddy reach his climax. (The marriage was annulled two days later. Frisco Freddy is now Fred Goldfarb, commercial real estate agent). It was all part of the adventure.

It seemed so normal; it was our existence. If we timed our chemicals right, we might peak during a terrific rendition of "Chalk Dust Torture" that would stoke college apartment discussions for weeks on end. My favorite moment/ lyric of any Phish show was in the same song, when Trey erupted into, "Can't this wait 'til I'm old? Can't I live while I'm young?!" That lyric was the unofficial catch phrase for my way of life.

The words were a true celebration of our freedom. Of being young, making our own bold choices and not wanting to face any of the responsibilities of the "real world".

When their concerts were announced, a plan was hatched to buy tickets and block out the dates on our calendars. We traveled anywhere, drove in any state of mind, and slept five deep on friends' apartment floors. It was all part of being twenty and being in love with a band of four vagrant virtuoso musicians from Vermont. Nothing could ever distance me from my brothers – the ones onstage and the ones in that endless, dancing crowd: the nameless faces who said to me, "Have a good show," before every gate opened, or the post-show strangers who would sell me a *Pheelin' Phine* sticker and a joint for ten bucks in the parking lot to help face the impending comedown on the drive home.

And then, something happened.

Around 1998, somewhere between college and the real world, something changed. I remember going to the July 20, 1998 show at the Ventura County Fairgrounds, and for the first time, at age 23, feeling as if the band and I had suddenly grown apart. Maybe it happened during "Poor Heart" when I didn't get up and dance like a maniac, or maybe it happened somewhere in the second set during "Maze" when I suddenly developed a bunch of insecurities about my career choices and lack of girlfriend; I was never quite sure. All I knew was that there was suddenly a grand abyss between us. I contemplated a drive to the following night's show at the Desert Sky Pavilion in Phoenix, the site of some of the most memorable concerts of my youth… and I decided against it. It somehow seemed a little irresponsible and desperate, like another distraction from chasing my new path.

Don't get me wrong, plenty of my friends attended and sent me letters telling me that they couldn't believe I missed my home state gig – but I somehow didn't care. (I think I saw Big Bad Voodoo Daddy at the Derby in Hollywood that same night and felt pretty damn good about myself.)

The recent passing of a dear friend, whom I had last seen at a Phish concert a year prior, cast a vague sorrowful cloud over the frivolity of my youth. It was as if a window of life had closed and a dream had ended. I sold Hayley's Comet that summer and bought a more sensible 1998 Honda CR-V. It went unnamed.

My final show was September 17, 1999 at Shoreline. I sort of wandered around during a long jam session in the second set, bored. It was as if the drug had worn off and I couldn't wait to get back to my room and climb into my bed. I was only 24 years old, but I had peaked. It was time to settle in, make some money and follow my own dreams of leading my own band – instead of just following someone else's.

When I finally got my band together in 2002, our goal was to outdraw Phish in five years…that didn't quite happen. (My band went on to some extremely minor success on the zombie country – rap music movie soundtrack circuit - but we never quite sold out Madison Square Garden.)

A year after my last show, Phish broke up. I felt like I had timed it perfectly. For six strong years, I had followed a band to the ends of the Earth, draining my wallet while feeding my head and my soul. I was 25 and engulfed by Hollywood, listening to new finds like The Band, Gram Parsons, and Little Feat. Suddenly, Phish seemed like a tiny speck on the musical map, and I was done with their guidance. The CD's and tapes began collecting dust as I opened my mind to a deeper tracklist of songs, only occasionally reminiscing about doing the clapping thing along with 13,000 people during songs like "Stash". The band had broken up, my hair had been cut off, and things like set lists and rides to shows no longer mattered. I didn't think I'd ever see Phish live again.

***

The phone call came two days before the concert. Our old friend Larry had bought four tickets to the 2012 West Coast summer tour kick-off show at the Long Beach Arena. His first instinct was to gather the tribe back together for a reunion show. It was brilliant. Larry had assembled a crew of former fraternity brothers and Phish-heads alike, none bigger than I, a man with nearly 35 shows to my name, including some as far back as 1993. Our pal Mike was coming, his first show since 1997. Also along for the ride was a man known as "The Sauce" (for his impressive drinking ability back in college), a longtime fan who had seen over 12 shows. And Larry. As advanced a partier as I have ever known, he was never without a pocketful of Percocet and a bottle of 18-year-old scotch in his back pocket. We were four old warriors returning for one more battle with the great gentle giant of our past. Prepared to run the place, the way we did in 1997; prepared to experience an earth-shattering, revolutionary moment of clarity, perhaps at a time when we all needed it the most.

All four of us are in our late 30's and married. Three of us have steady, high-paying jobs. I was the exception, still coasting along in the entertainment industry. Whereas we used to compare make-out stories and conquests, now there are nine children between the four of us. It was a far cry from smoking an ounce of weed in an old Ford Explorer with our sorority girlfriends.

Larry's offer was impossible to refuse.

I had actually broken my Phish hiatus a year earlier. The summer of 2011, I had gone to see Phish at the Hollywood Bowl, my first show in twelve years. It had blown my mind. The songs were familiar and inspiring, and even new jams like "Backwards Down the Number Line" had me believing for a few glorious hours that my previous life with the band had all been worth it. I hit peaks, flashed back to marvelous memories on highways and in hotels with girls and old friends, and eventually simmered into a state of serenity as I took a $5.00 cab ride home. I had never seen a more perfect concert. So, the possibilities a show in Long Beach held were endless. Old friends gathering once again in a beach community to smoke a little, drink a little, and dance a little? It was a no-brainer. I signed up immediately. Mike and the Sauce were in too. The stage was set. We would meet down at the Long Beach Hilton around 5:00 pm and pre-party before hitting the show. If all went too crazy, we'd share a hotel room. We'd even try to carpool down to save money for parking and gas. We were planning on spending a night not thinking about the troubles at work, our kid's schooling, or whether or not to sell our Facebook stock. Larry had even mentioned ecstasy. After a minute-long consideration, we all passed, but the knowing smiles we shared with each other reminded us of a time more innocent when rolling on a tab of E guaranteed a brilliant Phish experience. We decided to just have a few beers and maybe split a joint; we had grown up.

The 5:00 meeting did not happen. When work let out, the traffic to Long Beach from Los Angeles was unbearable. I left my house at 3:30 and met up with the Sauce at five. We then spent another hour and a half on the 405 and 710 to the LBC. It took us roughly three hours to get to the concert. I was fuming.

Back in the day, a two-day drive to Texas for a show would have never been out of the question. These days however, spending three hours in a car is not my idea of a "night out from the kids". And years ago, joints would have eased the pain of the ride as we blasted some live tape from 1992, smiling at the cars we crept along the freeway with. Now we were afraid to hold our cell phones up to our ears for fear of getting pulled over for not having "hands-free" devices.

The Sauce and I made a wrong turn off the 710, but somehow ended up meeting Mike and Larry at the hotel. After long-overdue friendly pleasantries were exchanged, we immediately started spotting members of the familiar Phish army. Kids showed up in John Fishman dresses – kooky Phish t-shirts from 30 years of merchandising gone right - and plenty of man-dals; it was all as familiar as a "Bathtub Gin" guitar riff. As we approached the venue, we became aware that we were definitely amongst the older generation – by at least 7-10 years. Instead of being the long-haired young kids with hot girlfriends, we were the dirty old dudes drooling over hot twenty-something hippie girls who were there with *their* boyfriends. It should also be noted that the hairy-armpitted girls of the 90's were nowhere to be seen. The California crowd was HOT. The dreadlocked smock-wearing wanderers who would hitch rides with us from town to town were gone.

I smoked a joint with my old friends. We laughed, shared pictures of our kids, and split decent gyros we bought from some dude on a bicycle. It started to feel like home once again. As we saw the throng of concertgoers celebrating the religious night, we all felt young and innocent again. We were transported back to a time of peace and incorruptibility, purity and clarity. We were in heaven.

I'm pretty sure I made my first mistake when I stood in a 30-minute line to get a wristband to buy beer; nobody had told me that inside, there was a smaller line. I also made the mistake of not using the Porta-Potties outside. I saw five people waiting to pee and got frustrated. But when I went inside, the line was 75 dudes deep; it took me another twenty minutes to hit the head.

Still, as the anticipation for the show mounted, the familiar feeling returned. I knew I was seeing one of my all-time favorite bands and I couldn't wait to get into the music like I had one year earlier at the Hollywood Bowl. It had been five hours since I left my house. I had drunk a few beers and took a long hit off another friend's chillum; I was flying high when they opened the show with "Suzy Greenberg", an old school jam that I used to LOVE. I hadn't even thought about the song in sixteen years, but it sounded as boisterous and thunderous as it had all those years ago. The set continued: "Kill Devil Falls" is one of my newest favorites. "Bouncing Round the Room" made me reminisce about old friends dancing around my apartment, just young and dumb and free…fucking FREE.

Back in the 90's, I would have been able to tell you what song was beginning by the first three notes. I knew every opening riff, line, bass thump, drum kick, you name it. Now, it took me half a song to even recognize what it was. Still, it didn't matter. That first set was perfect. We were all happily stoned, shrugging off the $10.50 Miller Lites, and ignoring the fact that the Long Beach Arena should really have been reserved for a WNBA game instead of a Phish concert in a fine-looking slice of California near the sea. Even the dozens of people near us smoking cigarettes didn't bother us just yet. We were all in a Phish trance, heckling stadium vendors trying to sell kettle corn and churros to a bunch of drugged-out superfans and doing our best to remember our killer dance moves.

Everything was conscious. Everyone was free. Everyone was happy…until they played "Stash". It was then that I decided to make my first journey onto my iPhone to see what the name of the song was. (Back in college I would have had the lyrics tattooed on my arm, but now, I was struggling with the title). As I looked at my phone, my wife's name appeared in a text. As did my brother's.

And a text from a possible business opportunity. Suddenly, Phish was GONE. I had to return my wife's text to make sure the kids were okay. I had to send my brother a PDF file. I had to go talk to my business contact about the TV show idea he had. I was distracted. I suddenly remembered it was Wednesday. Oh man, I had shit to do.

The classic "Stash" lyric "Was it for this my life I sought? Maybe so and maybe not" rang out.

It made sense when I was 20. It made perfect sense again.

I made sure I clapped at the right places and sang the "Ohhwooahh woah woah ooh" part in the song somewhat properly, albeit less enthusiastically than I had all those years ago, but I listened to that lyric repeat itself as I embarrassingly dove back into my phone. Afraid my friends would make fun of me for not being as entranced by the show as they were, I was pleasantly surprised to look over and see that Larry, Mike and the Sauce were all frantically texting on their phones as well. We were once slaves to the music. Now we were slaves to technology, wives, kids, and work.

I decided to wait to go outside to call my wife until after the first set, which was a good move. When Phish crushed the arena with "Quinn the Eskimo", I was as festive as anyone my age can get. As I drooled over some ridiculously hot dancing brunette who reminded me of half the girls I had dated in the 90's, I began whispering to my friends about how old I felt at the show. We all nodded, laughed and high-fived.

I think The Sauce was the first one of us to yawn.

I knew I had to go find a quiet place where I could calmly call my wife in peace and let her know I wasn't wasted, and that I would be home on time to wake up with the kids so she could go to work in the morning. As the set ended and the place erupted, I darted for the doors. Somehow, I beat the bathroom line and even got a beer before getting stuck in the sweat-filled traffic towards the front entrance where a full cell phone signal awaited. I called. It rang. My wife was asleep. I looked at the time: 9:45 p.m. Once, it would have been the beginning of my evening. Now? It was fucking *late.*

I looked at all the fans around me. Most of them were texting, tweeting and updating Facebook pages, which I chalk up to the generation. However, when I saw the crew I had rolled with come outside, it was thoroughly predictable. We were all blowing kisses to our wives, checking on kids and even taking business calls. (Larry opened and closed a lawsuit between sets.)

The Sauce took a ten-minute business phone call.

Mike went off to buy a churro and didn't return for forty minutes.

I sent photos of the crowd to my brother.

The guy next to me played Angry Birds.

Thirty minutes later, we were all exhausted and ready to call it a night. Still, we forced ourselves back inside. The anticipation had come and gone, and the reality of an hour-long drive back to LA sank in as we all crowded around the water fountains for free cups of polluted tap water, just to avoid the overpriced Dasani's from the concession stands.

As we sat in our seats, the lights came back and an unfamiliar tune came on. After five minutes of pretending we knew what it was, a guy behind us finally used the "Shazam" app on his phone and figured out it was "Rock and Roll" by The Velvet Underground. The Phish version went on for 25 minutes. It was amazing. But then…the PDF file I had sent earlier didn't go through. Larry's lawsuit took a turn for the worse. The Sauce had to discuss hotel design with somebody in Macau. Mike's churro sucked. We were no longer the four Phish phreaks who would bed five girls before the night was through. We were grown men with responsibilities and allergies, children and long drives home. We were fading fast. When "Ghost" started, I shrugged it off. It was never one of my favorite songs, but I knew it well. It was one of the songs I remembered from when I began to separate myself from the band. Still, it sounded great, and my body seemed to once again start buzzing…until I realized it was just the buzz from another text from my wife. Our two-year-old daughter was awake and crying. I felt guilty for not being there.

I'm pretty sure I was the second one to yawn.

Larry soon informed me during "Guyute" that he had a place for me to crash on his hotel room floor. My contact lenses were burning and the drive home seemed impossible, but I figured at my age it would be better to get home rather than wake up in Long Beach and hitch a ride back to Hollywood. I decided to go get some water from the tap once again. After four glasses I was in the bathroom, staring at the bags below my eyes in the mirror while listening to two twenty-something kids discuss some festival in 2008 that I had obviously missed. I heard "Guyute" climax into that Space Age three chord rebirth that always made me happy, and I smiled again. I was back inside, full of energy and ideas and resilience and glee…until I returned to find a good amount of the fans in my section seated and nearly unconscious with boredom.

"I'm bouncing like a newborn elf," sang Trey.

Really? I didn't see any newborn elves dancing near me. I saw four guys who were exhausted, rubbing their temples and beginning to worry about their hearing.

I stuck it out for "Julius" – one of my all time favorites – but when I noticed that our crew was all in the wife-texting mode we all looked at each other with an unspoken knowledge that it was time to go home. Yes, we had blossomed into the OLD GUYS AT THE PHISH SHOW. We weren't quite what we used to be. And I think, truthfully, we were all a little grateful that we weren't.

I remember waiting in line to buy Phish t-shirts as a kid to wear around college and try and instigate conversation. I made it a ceremonial task to buy a shirt at every show I went to. I have something like 22 Phish t-shirts in a closet in my house and I'll hold onto them forever. Mike, Sauce, Larry and I thought we'd take a look at the newest merch and maybe drop a few bills. Of course, the only items that appealed to us were the baby onesies. Mike bought a toddler t-shirt and a newborn onesie. Larry got a onesie as well. I decided against it, as my kids were a little older, but it was the final moment of truth. The thrill had faded fast.

It was the first time I had ever left before the encore. It was the first time I was happy to do so. It was the first time I hadn't bought a beer, a burrito, or weed in the post-show parking lot. It was the first time I hadn't left completely blasted out of my skull.

When Mike suggested taking a taxi back to the hotel three blocks away, all four of us smiled. Yes, a taxi! Brilliant! We were close enough to walk, but forget that idea, man. When we arrived at the Hilton, we split the $5.25 charge, said some pleasant good-byes and split apart. We had done what we came to do… sort of. It was a new experience on an old battlefield; we were the decorated aging generals of yore.

On the drive home from Long Beach, I fired up the MP3 player to "Chalk Dust Torture." There was that magical phrase again:

"Can't this wait 'til I'm old, Can't I live while I'm young…"

Well, I guess I let it wait 'til I was old. I lived when I was young! And even though 37 still seems young in a way, when there are babies to feed and diapers to change at 6:00 in the morning, it can also feel really fucking old.

Still, Phish will forever inhabit a deep piece of my heart – and should they play anywhere within 100 miles of me I will go anytime. The band is one of the reasons why I became a confident stage performer, a songwriter, and a well-traveled man. They were a part of my youth, but are also part of my adulthood. They continue to offer inspiration and wild creativity, and they also continue to keep me grounded. I know that nothing lasts forever, be it friendships, bands, trends, beauty, money, you name it. All we have is belief, love, and music. And that ain't bad at all.

Born Yesterday

In 1951, my grandfather was approached by an entrepreneur asking him if he would like to invest in an upstart hamburger chain that would, "Change the way Americans eat forever." Undaunted by the sales pitch, my grandfather denied putting any of his hard earned money into the place, and offered the following sentence that will forever haunt my family:

"Why would anybody ever wanna buy a cheap hamburger when they can just have their wife cook them a nice steak at home?"

That upstart hamburger chain became McDonald's. A partner in my grandfather's dental practice who had invested owned half of Manhattan within five years… My grandfather filled cavities until he was 70.

So, when a guy who I met briefly at a friend's wedding ten years ago called me out of the blue this week and asked me if I was ready to turn my life upside down, I perked up. At first, I thought he was going to ask me to read his screenplay or to listen to his reality TV pitch, but instead he started selling me on the thousands of acres of unclaimed natural beach-front property that was available for purchase down in Nicaragua. After explaining that the *Contras* had long been dormant and that this country was "the next Mexico," he texted me pictures of the three beachfront lots he owned on the edge of paradise before asking me if I'd like to invest in this incredible business opportunity.

I told him to piss off.

To all of the sewer-toiling gutter rats who have tried to get me into some sort of rancid, imbecilic, brainwashed pyramid scheme at anytime throughout the past 15 years… I am not interested. Get off my Facebook. Stop texting me. Don't invite me to your seminar. Ain't gonna happen.

From the original lecherous late 90's Amway assholes to today's "one pill will make you healthy and muscular… all while lowering your weight and boosting your metabolism and energy" jackals of today – I've HAD IT. Stop. I'm not going to sell your stupid product. I don't care about Monavie or Isagenix or the God damn Proto-Cookie. Keep your brochures.

I am not buying land in Nica-fucking-ragua.

The first time I was introduced to the "get rich quick" world was when an old fraternity brother named Tommy Decker wrangled 15 of my friends - all recent college graduates - into a Hollywood living room during the summer of 1998. Somehow, we had all failed to become millionaires one year out of college and found ourselves living off of cans of tuna fish, day-old bread and deli samples from the grocery store. Girls were few and far between. Everything looked dreary and bleak… and we realized there was a tough climb ahead… Rich guys got all the chicks.

So when Tommy Decker and I crossed paths at Canter's Deli late one night, he began preaching about his new company that was going to be able to make my buddies and I very rich for simply getting our friends and family to switch to a new company for home service known as *Quickstar*. (Named change to avoid any future death threats…) He bought me a few drinks and asked for a simple favor. All Tommy wanted was for me to get some pals to come to a meeting the next night where a whole new world of opportunity awaited.

Turns out, Tommy also wanted a 500-dollar up front investment to get each of us started as employees in his company. He also wanted a commitment that we would convince the greater Los Angeles area that Quickstar was a better home phone company than MCI or Bell – or whatever the main provider was at the time.

The following evening, I managed to gather 14 friends and we all met at an impressive mid-century house in West Hollywood where cheese squares and yellow crackers were served alongside sparkling water and Coca-Cola. It wasn't much, but to four broke guys sharing a two-bedroom duplex, the house was certainly impressive.

And then the presentation began.

Throughout the meeting, Tommy fastidiously declared that Quickstar was "not a pyramid scheme." Instead, explained how the money in the company flowed through the structure less like a "pyramid," and more like a "triangular scepter."

Tommy used big, inflated words and ultimately promised us all exponential bonuses and benefits as the business began to expand. He electrified us with big numbers and the neat graphics – and used a really interesting analogy of something he referred to as the "train conductor layout." Essentially, He was the "Conductor" of the train. He had two guys beneath him known as "Car Captains," 15 guys below him known as the "Baggage Porters" and them the newest guys – like us – who would be referred to as the "Coal Shovelers." (At least until we were able to sell enough to become "Baggage Porters.")

I didn't quite like the idea of being a "Coal Shoveler," but at least it seemed easy and Tommy convinced me it would only be a quick stint in the coal car before I was promoted to the luggage rack. After all, according to him, I had the perfect personality for this kind of work.

The true kicker for me was when Tommy finally introduced us to *his* Conductor, a clean-cut and handsome chap named Joey. Joey was a mid-30's cheese dick who drove a BMW 5 Series and bragged about his house in Tarzana with a tennis court. He claimed to have a loft in New York, two homes in wine country and a piece of the Chicago Bears. He mentioned that he had been backstage to see the *Rolling Stones* and that Ron Wood signed on as a Quickstar participant. He also flashed a 30,000-dollar Rolex and spoke of his yacht and off-shore bank accounts.

All of which -he claimed - was made by turning folks onto *Quickstar.*

He showed us some slides on an overhead projector (The first iPad) and told us we all had bright futures. He guaranteed we'd be making ten thousand dollars a month within weeks before reporting that he was due back at the Chateau Marmont for a date with a Victoria Secret's supermodel at eleven.

I completely bought it.

I was in. Even though I had about 1000 dollars in my checking account, I cut a check that night and went home the next day to begin my reign as the lord of Quickstar home phone communications.

The smart ones laughed and walked away.

Like my roommate, Mike.

And a kid named Yael.

A guy named Kirk who demanded that Joey take him to the Chateau to meet this Victoria Secret girl. When he was denied, Joey explained it was only because she was *really, really famous.* I went home and slept soundly, envisioning myself cashing five-figure monthly checks before squiring some lingerie model off to a Sunset Strip hotel for a night of expensive spirits and romance. The future looked marvelous.

I got my welcoming packet in the mail a few days later.

The Quickstar formula was as follows: You had to convince everyday MCI, Bell and AT& T subscribers to switch their home phone service to the newer, cheaper Quickstar service. All it took was asking them to share their credit card numbers with a total stranger and to commit to a twelve-month rate plan. The people could keep their old phone numbers and everything. Hey, it was cheaper, right? Who *wouldn't* go for this incredible deal?

Turns out a lot of people.

Within 24 hours, I was certified as a Quickstar salesman and I was issued a "Coal Shoveler Number" that I had to enter into every successful transaction I pulled off. I was sent a cheap golf shirt with the Quickstar logo and about 750 sheets of paper that outlined in full detail everything I would be selling my new minions. They recommended that we read all of the fine print before starting our sales pitches, but I had no time for that. I was ready to get rich…I hit the warpath on the first day of August 1998 – convincing myself that a windfall of cash awaited me and that I would be able to write thousands of contracts daily. I started on Melrose Avenue – hitting the cheap retail stores.

Huge mistake.

Most of the Melrose Avenue store owners were of Israeli and Iranian descent. When they saw a little white kid with a James Dean haircut enter their store and try to convince them to switch their phone service over to Quickstar, they didn't exactly welcome me. My one lead came from a cute waitress at the Johnny Rockets restaurant who, after hearing my spiel, convinced me to order a 15-dollar hamburger, French fries and milkshake.

She never called me back.

That weekend, I tried to convince everybody at my work to switch over, but most of them didn't wasn't to go through the hassle of canceling their old service and filling out three pages of paperwork. The office of Disc Jockey's I was a part of was so busy at the time, they explained that the dollar amount I was offering them in savings didn't make sense for a business with over 25 working land lines. They had some bulk deal going with Bell or something. Once again, I was unable to close any deals.

Growing frustrated, my next few moves were made on my buddies up and down the Hollywood landscape, sharing apartments littered in beer cans and pizza boxes, hoping they would be grateful to save $6.95 a month on *anything*. Unfortunately, a lot of these guys were either using stolen phone card numbers to make long distance calls and others had their phone bills paid by their fathers… so there was no way they were going to get me his credit card information.

After six days on the job, I had made absolutely zero headway.

It was then that I called my grandmother.

My grandma is now 90-years-old and still somewhat sharp, although the years may be finally catching up to her. Back in 1998, she was 76 and as spry, caring and lively as any person could be. My grandfather was still alive and they were enjoying their retirement with long desert walks in Tucson, riding in their vintage Cadillac and steak and scotch dinners nearly nightly. They were also willing to do anything for me.

I made the call to my grandma on day seven. I told her I had landed a "new job," and that I was going to be very rich and successful if I could just get a few people to switch their phone plans over to Quickstar. I went through the business plan and said it was a "no-brainer." I explained how she could save $6.95 a month and told her about Tommy's success and how these guys all believed I had what it took to make a lot of money in this business.

My grandmother responded by simply asking me one question.

"What do you think, I was born yesterday?"

She broke down the scheme for me. She tossed off stories about friends of hers from the 1940's through the 80's who had fallen for pyramid schemes, 'Matrix schemes,' Multi-Level Marketing, "franchise churning" and a whole bunch of other ridiculous get-rich quick proposals that blew up in their faces. One friend of grandpas had in fact, committed suicide in the 70's after falling for a snake-oil swindler and his investment opportunity. She was clearly upset that I had been recruited into this little Quickstar cult and expressed severe disappointment in my inability to spot a rip-off con game when it as first presented to me.

I simply responded by saying, "This one is different."

My grandmother changed the subject and asked when I was coming home to visit. I said I'd be home in the fall, and told her I hadn't forgotten her wedding anniversary and that I'd be sending a card in the next day or two. She smiled, told me she loved me and once again demonstratively expressed her worry about this Quickstar program I was involved in.

I dug deep into my emotional handbag and told her that she had nothing to worry about. She said she did. I told her to relax. She told me to not be a fool. I took a deep breath and spent the next 45 seconds in silence.

I then calmly asked my grandma for her credit card number.

For some reason she gave it to me.

Thinking that I was the world's greatest salesman, I leapt for joy in my apartment. I told my Grandma she wouldn't be disappointed and mentioned that I would be taking her out for lunch in the next few months. She sighed, said "I love you and be careful" and then we hung up.

Looking back now, my grandma is so loving and sweet, I could have probably sold her on funding a Nazi Youth rally… but at the time, it was my first sale and I was convinced that I was on my way.

Ecstatic, I filled out the paperwork and prepared to submit my first sale to Tommy and Joey – knowing that it was only a matter of time before I was making it rain at some strip club with my newfound riches…When I left them messages, they didn't respond.

The next day they didn't respond either. Nor did I hear from them on day three. I had sent in the paperwork, as requested, but nobody had reached back out to me. It seemed strange, but I figured I just had to keep signing up customers and I would become a "Conductor" in no time…Instead, I got a call from my mom two nights later claiming that grandma's credit card had been charged $500 for switching to some new phone company called "Quickstar."

If you're reading this and you were born after 1982, you must remember that the internet was not even around at this time. Sure, there were chat rooms and dial up modems that took about nine days to register, but information was not as readily available as it is today. (In fact, I once spent an entire week with a girl trying to figure out who sang the 80's dance song "Pure Energy.")

Information Society, if you're interested.

So basically, I had no idea what any of this stuff was. There were no warning signs and no websites and no Yelp and no people telling you to avoid this kind of pyramid scam online. All we had were our *grandmothers*, warning us against the perils of buying into this kind of get rich quick crap… and I had gone and completely ignored mine for the sake of a quick sale.

When Tommy finally got back to me, he claimed that the Quickstar folks had suddenly been audited and that things were at a standstill. I told him that my poor, aging grandmother was about to have a heart attack over this mysterious 500-dollar charge. Tommy apologized for the delay and that he was sorry. He also noted that the fine print on the welcome package revealed the 500-dollar start up charge for switching companies… it was apparently in the 750-page packet I had declined to read. Tommy also mentioned that he was considering jumping ship…and he recommended I do the same.

When I asked him to be honest with me and tell me the truth, he simply said, "I can't go into it right now."

So there I was, 500 dollars poorer. Worst of all, so was my innocent grandma. Even worse than that was that she had warned me of this kind of thing happening. I sunk into my bed for the next two days, leaving my place only for work and for runs to get beer at he local market. I was humiliated and embarrassed.

Even my roommate Mike gave me the old, "I told you so."

A few days later, I finally decided to use my developing acting skills to do what I was always able to do better than most any person I ever knew… Convince somebody I had been ripped off. It was time to lie.

I called my bank and claimed I had a check stolen out of my mailbox for $500. I said it was a payment to my student loans and they had yet to receive it. When the bank told me that a check with the coinciding numbers had been cashed for 500 dollars, I demanded to have it revoked and discarded. The woman told me that was impossible, especially because the bank had a record of an image of the check made out to a company called "Quickstar Integration Communication Services."

"What the hell is that?!" I screamed.

Claiming that I had been scammed, the lady took a look at the check image and said it didn't look forged, but said that there were a growing number of check fraud cases and identity theft rings on the new "world wide web." After forcing myself to shed "my life is over" tears over the phone, she finally agreed to reverse the payment and refund the money into my account. She also mentioned that I had to pay a small stop charge on the check, but I didn't care.

Victory: ME.

My next call was to my Grandmother's credit card company. I told them that somebody had been using my name as an "identity thief" and was ripping off little old ladies all across the country. They said they hadn't heard of the scheme, but I told them to contact my bank for confirmation. They called. The stolen check story was told and the charges were reversed. My grandma had her 500 dollars back.

My final order of business in my strange *Kill Bill* revenge story was to track down this "conductor" known as Joey. He had appeared only once, to show off his BMW and talk about his wicked backhanded tennis game, but since then he had not been heard of. I wondered who he was and why the hell he hadn't been around since the day I sent my check to the people of Quickstar. Unfortunately, my research led to dead end after dead end. Even Tommy said he hadn't heard from him in weeks and that the last he knew, Joey was in Puerto Vallarta with Claudia Schiffer.

I never saw or heard from Joey again.

The last time I saw Tommy he was producing content in the adult film business.

I continued to follow the Quickstar stories developing in the newspapers. They were notoriously audited and the company was also involved in numerous accounting scandals. They were fined $250 million by the U.S. Securities and Exchange Commission (SEC), and even had something to do with helping Enron conceal losses a few years later. Several employees were accused of fraud and insider trading in a civil lawsuit filed by the SEC.

My grandfather died in 2000. I begged my Grandma to never tell him what I had fallen into - and she had kept her promise. She was so relieved that I actually got her the money back, she eventually revealed to me that she had only signed up with Quickstar hoping to teach me a valuable lesson about trust and common sense.

I learned it well.

Today, every once in awhile, I have friends in Hollywood who get caught up in the schemes of the day. The pyramid structures are long gone, but the team building structures are EVERYWHERE. Especially online. I have been offered miracle youth pills, Better Beach Body DVD's, super protein drinks, revitalizing tonics, sporto-cookies, Isagenix, Cryogenix and all kinds of genix, Capsiplex slimming pills, HGH, River stone therapies… you name it. Ever since I got on television, people just start showing up. There is always some professional athlete who has invested big dollars and gives the brand a little credibility, but I have never once in my life seen an average Joe get rich off of selling a mysterious health product to strangers. All I have seen are guys who plaster their cars with stickers reading "HerbalLife" driving around town selling people, well… HerbaLife. You will probably have a better chance at getting rich by responding to those random emails from African Princes who need your bank account number to deposit the 45 billion dollars you are entitled to.

So whenever a friend emails me with a "business opportunity," I immediately tell them to email me the information and quickly delete it. Sometimes I call my grandmother and tell her about whatever ridiculous scheme has been presented to me and we spend some time laughing off the old Quickstar story from all those years ago.

When the Nicaraguan beachfront opportunity was presented, I humored my old friend and clicked on some photos of the investment property. For 25,000 dollars, one could own such a beautiful slice of Nicaraguan heaven overlooking the pristine Caribbean Sea. It actually was pretty gorgeous. It seemed cheap and somewhat breathtaking. For a minute, I considered making it my new home by the sea.

I did some further research and found that for as little as $500 a month, I could actually be *living* in this dream palace – sipping tropical drinks and counting sailboats as the Central American sun submerged itself into the placid blue, spraying a watercolor sunset across my hammock-lined beachfront porch.

Suddenly intrigued, I did some further Google-searching and saw even more photos of white sandy beaches, tanned bronze-skinned beauties rippling through barely-there bikinis and glimmering modern-day pirates drinking rum-infused umbrella drinks surrounded by Spanish guitars.

I was about to call my grandmother to help me invest.

But then, I happened upon one final scathing review of the properties that were being offered and the types of people living in the area. One investor described it as, "Nothing like the brochures and sunsets I was presented – just minutes from the house I purchased, I encountered a very filthy, noisy, city. Utter anarchy… This was a huge mistake and Nicaragua is a virtual hell on earth."

I came to the conclusion that investing in Nicaraguan beachfront was not such a great idea. After all, I wasn't born yesterday…

The Sobriety Journal

On December 28, 2012, during a visit to my in-laws' house for Christmas, I took my family to a Chuck E. Cheese in Poulsbo, Washington. After receiving the proper guardian safety stamps, slathering my body with hand sanitizer, and shelling out $40 for three cups of tokens, I noticed that behind the counter, above a small chemistry lab sink in a non-descript homemade metal serving area that looked like a sink from my high school chemistry class, were four taps reading, "CHABLIS, BLUSH, RED and LIGHT BEER". Being in a Chuck E. Cheese in the Pacific Northwest, I had to inquire about the beer and wine they were serving; their display looked like something out of a Prohibition-era speakeasy. Despite this, I was feeling a little on edge, and 300 screaming kids sneezing and running all around Chuck E. Cheese seemed a lot easier to deal with should I have a pitcher of beer on hand.

I inquired about buying a pitcher of the light beer, but was told that the keg was kicked. The young lady behind the counter recommended the "Red". I told her I didn't want any wine, but as it turned out the "Red" was not red wine, but a local "red brew" from nearby Silverdale with an extremely high alcohol content. I ordered up a pitcher, paid the young lady another $14.00, and went off to challenge some nine-year-olds to a Pop-a-Shot tournament.

Following a 45-16 drubbing at the hands of a 12-year-old named Jayden, I sunk into our family booth and proceeded to pound three of these red beers in under an hour. Suddenly, I felt like I was a 12-year-old at a friend's birthday party in 1987. I was engulfed by the dazzling lights and sounds of the Chuck E. Cheese. I chased strange kids around the game room in a game of tag, took my daughter up into the plastic maze/slide and let a bunch of kids tackle me. and sat and posed for dumb pictures with my family and a giant stuffed mouse on a cheap amusement ride; I was truly the Superdad of the Chuck E. Cheese. My wife smiled at me as I approached her with a wad of gum stuck in my hair and a pizza sauce stain on my t-shirt.

"You really are the best dad," she said before kissing me.

As my buzz began to fade, I knew I would have to get another beer before we went home to keep the ride going. Deciding to skip dinner due to the plasticene appearance of the so-called pizza, I took down two more Reds and packed up the diaper bag. My son ended up winning 498 tickets, which he traded in for a stuffed mini-SpongeBob and a pencil, two pieces of unadulterated crap that retail for somewhere around 75 cents. I didn't care, though; it was a great time, and he had a blast playing all of the games and winning tickets. Best of all, I was leaving Chuck E. Cheese with a tremendous buzz and a newfound love for dark beer from the Pacific Northwest.

That was the last thing I remembered from that evening.

The next day I woke up around 10 a.m. to hear my wife cursing me out from the other room. She was saying something about me falling off the bed in the middle of the night and waking up our daughter. Having no recollection of this, I stumbled to my feet and looked helplessly for my eyeglasses. When I couldn't find them, I made a point of acting as if nothing was wrong, despite what felt like a million tiny five-year-olds thumping around inside my skull.

"You're in trouble," she said to me, glaring as I walked into the kitchen.

Her mother laughed. I squinted, only able to register the blurry shapes of my kids as they sat eating cereal and playing with their new Hannukkah and Christmas toys.

"What are you talking about?" I asked.

"Do you not remember what you *did* last night?" she offered.

"Oh, you mean when you told me I was the *best dad ever*?"

"I can't even look at you right now."

And with that I ran off to the bathroom, where I threw up a geyser of fluid and a distinctly unfamiliar mystery meat. I found my eyeglasses in the wastebasket by the toilet.

According to my in-laws, we had come home after Chuck E. Cheese and I had split a bottle of red wine with my wife's dad. When his neighbor Mike invited us over for some homemade beer and pork pozole, we both accepted.

My wife informed me that I had arrived at the door three hours later with my pants around my ankles. I was slurring and proceeded to pop my contact lenses out of my eyeballs and throw them across the room. After nearly falling through a plate glass window and severing my carotid artery, *I demanded that my wife turn on a porno film on the big screen television*, before yelling at my mother-in-law to "go the hell to bed already". I passed out on the couch and was carried to bed by my wife and her dad.

When this was all relayed to me by my wife, who just hours earlier had been commending me on my parenting skills, I let the situation slowly sink in. As I attempted to keep down some coconut water and wiped the never ending sweat from my brow, I began to think that it might be a good time to take a closer look at what *WebMD* had described as "my drinking problem".

I spent the rest of the day in bed or in the bathroom, vomiting. It was one of the worst feelings I have ever experienced; it was not unlike those 24-hour bugs that have been going around where you puke and sleep forever, convinced you are dying. I hated every minute of it, especially because I was incapable of playing with my kids due to the pain. Embarrassed and ashamed, I took a vow of sobriety on the afternoon of December 29, 2012. I also vowed to chronicle my efforts in my journals, which I had been fastidiously keeping since my 16th birthday but had grown a little lazy about recently. I was sort of hoping that my abstinence would re-inspire me to keep a more comprehensive diary again; but instead of logging activities and hours in the following pages, I mainly focused on the extremely difficult task of avoiding alcohol at all costs.

What follows is lifted directly from my personal journal beginning the day of December 29th and continuing on until I broke my streak. I hope this either inspires you to face your demons head on, or to continue drinking responsibly so you do not end up trying to turn on a DVD of *Little Orphan Anal* in front of your wife's parents over the holidays.

Sobriety Journal. Aka The Non-Rum Diary.

December 29, 2012

Day 1: OOOOOOOhhhh God. I have been puking for nine hours straight and I don't even have any food in my body… I think I just threw up knee cartilage. Last night was a lost bender of epic proportions, coming to a head at the neighbor's house (Mike? Mark?) where I drank his homemade 14% alcohol Belgian Tripelbock after killing six beers and some wine during and before dinner. I don't remember the end of the night, but the wife said I arrived at the in-laws' door with my pants around my ankles. My last memory was beer at Chuck E. Cheese – and my kids playing arcade games with those disease-ridden tokens. All I found was this picture crumpled up in my wallet of me slamming a beer with my finger up my nose.

Shit, maybe I got roofied. Roofeed? How do you spell that?

December 30, 2012

Day 2: Wow, the day after hangover. Maybe I'll have a bowl of Honey smacks and watch *Breaking Bad* on DVD all day... Wife is in the other room talking about going to the mall or something. Not me. I'm still laid up... No more booze, ever. Period. I'm serious. 100%. Even though it's New Year's Eve in two days and we're invited to a party in LA thrown by the guy who owns the Coldwater Wine Company, I will refrain... It's been fifteen years of this shit; time to grow up and be a man. Fuck it, man... Robert Downey Jr. got sober. So did Dick Van Dyke and Richard Dreyfus and Nick Nolte...I think... Maybe even Slash... wait, is Slash sober? If Slash is sober, I can be sober. Although I only seem to over consume wine and beer . . . I think Slash was mainlining jet fuel at one point... I don't know... I don't want to have to keep explaining myself, especially once my kids are old enough to wonder why daddy is staying in bed all day. I talked to George Carlin's daughter Kelly once; she told me she spent every morning of her childhood wondering when her parents would wake up and play with her... Apparently they had a blackout curtain in their room to keep out that evil sun. Luckily, I'm in Washington State right now and the sun is nowhere to be found. We go home tomorrow. . .thank GOD.

(15 minutes later)

My wife's brother just brought over a six pack and a bottle of wine and I turned him down! I think I'm cured! Who needs Dr. Drew? Fuck that guy! I will never crave booze again!

December 31, 2102

Day 3: I want booze. So badly. Just some wine or a beer or something… DAMN! And it's New Year's Eve! What the hell. I'm so exhausted. We're invited to about three different parties but I don't want to go to any of them. I'm probably gonna do the lame West Coast dad thing and watch the ball drop at 9 pm on an East Coast feed…that is very, very sad. Two years ago I took ecstasy and covered myself in body paint with a crowd of naked strangers in an apartment in Glendale. Yeah, I was in a shithole in Glendale and I was on ecstasy and I felt like I was being licked by the tongue of God. It was awesome. Now, I'm two nights sober. My head feels cloudy and my body is still in shock...maybe it was the pint of Ben and Jerry's Phish Food I consumed last night in an effort to curb my body's sugar cravings, who the hell knows. It is 8:31 at night and I don't even think I can make it to New York New Year's…so I am signing off, asleep at 8:34 on New Year's Eve.

Jan. 1, 2013

Day 4: I feel a lot better! Might even attempt to go to the gym and run today, but I don't know. We're invited to a friend's house for football and wine later and they always have the best French Bourdeaux. How the hell does that happen? Man, when you are not drinking, THE WHOLE WORLD IS AN OPEN BAR!!!

(Later that night)

I just told my wife I had a late night meeting, but in reality, I'm off to the grocery store to buy some more ice cream. Seriously. I am lying to my wife so that I can go eat a pint of Ben and Jerry's in the Gelson's parking lot. Alone. Jesus. Some men have affairs, I sneak off to have sex with pints of Cherry Garcia.

January 2, 2013

Day 5: Back to the gym, finally sweat out the remnants of that night. I smelled like a beer on the treadmill. It was sad. My mom and my grandma fly in later tonight. My mom will immediately wonder why I am not drinking. She is a two-bottles-of-Chardonnay-a-night drinker. I normally stay up with her and talk, but this might be the time I don't. Damn! I love drinking with my mom!

January 3, 2013

Day 6: My mom and I had this conversation last night beginning at about 4:45 in the afternoon:

MOM: "Why aren't you drinking?"

ME: "I had a rough night last week and I'm taking some time off."

MOM: "You loser! Open some red wine and play Scrabble with me."

Somehow, I managed to not drink with her and I went to bed early instead. The last thing my mom said to me before she went to bed was, "I really hope this isn't a permanent thing. Think of your mother, won't you?"

I will say, my mom is one of my all time favorite drinking buddies. We sit and play old records and run through Scrabble games until two in the morning, usually forgetting to finish because we both get so loopy that we begin placing words like "oughta" on the board and accepting them. Meanwhile, my grandma, who is 90-years-old and still sharp and hilarious said to me, "I don't care if you stop drinking forever… you NEED to stop biting your nails!"

I love my grandma.

Jan. 4, 2013

Day 7: One week! Wow, I went one week. I still haven't found much inspiration to write or play guitar or anything, but my son and I played his new *Wreck it Ralph* Wii game for five hours straight today! Not that playing video games is productive, but it was something, right? Oh man, I sound like all the stoner gamer geeks I used to work with at G4. So that's what sobriety leads to? VIDEO GAMES? Shit, I might as well go get a bottle of Jim Beam right now. BTW, my mom and grandma went to Orange County to visit my sister, so I'm back to exercising and reading this great book on Bonnie and Clyde. Makes me happy I never shot anybody.

January 5, 2013

Day 8: OK, I was at a film screening tonight and they had an open bar. I had sparkling water with lemon, but I was craving alcohol. You know how we Jews are, anything free, we WANT IT!! Especially the red wines they had…

and the Pilsner beer… Oh, man. Anyway, I ended up drinking my first Coke in about five years. It was like drinking a Snickers bar. Jesus. I switched to Diet Coke, but my buddy Eric told me about all the studies and the chemicals and the fact that Diet Coke causes cancer and depression. My God. Once again, I'm better off drinking.

Jan 6. 2013

Day 9: Well, I just bought a six pack of Buckler non-alcoholic beer. It tastes alright, but is definitely lacking the sweet, calming effect of alcohol. I cracked one about two hours ago and drank it within three minutes. I drank the second one three minutes later. I killed the six pack in 28 minutes. Now I feel bloated and somewhat satisfied, as if there was a placebo affect to the whole thing. Whatever the case, my mom comes back tomorrow and I have an audition for a Toyota Commercial. I've also lost seven pounds.

January 7, 2013

Day 10: Fuck fuck fuck you Q Q Q Q DICK. Fucking dick fuck fuck this sucks fuck you dick dick balls dick.

January 8, 2013.

Day 11: FUCCCKKKKKK YOOOUUUU!UU!U!UU!U!U! I want a drink I want a drink I want a drink drink drink dnrindinrindikkkkkk. I texted a few sober friends and asked them how they deal with all of this and they sent me back the clichés we are all familiar with: *Cigarettes and coffee…meetings…ice cream…* My one buddy, a former coke-monkey named Bobby wrote *Dude, substitute one addiction for the other…why do you think I got divorced? I'm a cooze hound!*

January 9, 2013

Day 12: I have officially crossed the threshold! I truly believe I may not ever have a craving again. I'm exercising, nailing my auditions (Toyota callback!) and I've slowed down on my Ben and Jerry's to half a pint a night! This is the beginning of a whole new me! I will write tomorrow. I LOVE this!!

***

That was my final entry into the *Sobriety Journal.*

I made it twelve full days before being invited to a party where they were serving Johnnie Walker Blue Label and Sea Smoke red wine. I looked at my wife, who knew that the minute I saw the Sea Smoke (my favorite) I would be done for. She grabbed me and looked me in my eyes.

"Look, Zach," she said. "If you think you can have just a couple of glasses, I think you should. But *remember,* drink water, stay in control, and you don't have to *pound* the wine. Enjoy it, sip it, you know?"

I looked into my wife's sweet face. She was sticking by my side no matter what I did and I loved her for it. I knew she was my rock, my confidant, my unofficial "sponsor" if you will. The fact that she trusted me to know my limits meant more to me than anything in the entire world at that moment. I kissed her and promised to be responsible and careful as I watched her walk away into the party to hang with a group of women who were discussing their unnecessary scarves in the 60-degree Los Angeles winter night.

I rolled up to the bar and took a long hard moment to gather myself. The waiter poured me a decent glass of Sea Smoke and told me to enjoy it. I swirled the red lava around in the glassware like a vinyl record, letting it settle a few times before placing my nose up to its sublime aroma. I inhaled deeply, taking in the fine grape. This was GOOOD wine. The best wine to break a fortnight of sobriety with. I slowly pressed the glass to my lips and swallowed the heavenly liquid until my body turned warm with familiarity and melted into a séance-like calmness. I felt alive. I knew I was going to be able to conquer this demon and practice the finest art of them all: the art of *moderation.*

The next morning I woke up on the bathroom floor, fully clothed in the fetal position. I had no idea where my eyeglasses were.

647 Dollars and 97 Cents

In February of this past year, I traveled to New York City and somehow spent $647.97 in just under twelve hours, and I have absolutely nothing to show for it.

New York has always been one of my favorite cities; from the first time my mother took me as a kid to look at the Macy's holiday window displays, to the nights spent out eating at fabulous restaurants like Trattoria Del'Arte, to the time I urinated in a Yankee Stadium phone booth after a tough loss to the Blue Jays, New York City has enchanted me for all these years. And will continue to do so for the rest of my life.

Still, for all of New York's charm and romance, the place has sabotaged my wallet time and time again. No matter how hard I try to keep my expenditures under budget, I fail miserably every time.

Last February, I was flown out to New York to read a short story at a start-up literary festival called the "New Poets and Writers Rooftop Recital". I anticipated a catered event full of accomplished writers, sexy New York celebrities like Uma Thurman, and dozens of opportunities presenting themselves at every sip of champagne. It was the literary Mecca of the world and I was there to take it by storm; or at least, to try and get my stories printed in a respectable magazine. After all, my last published work had appeared in the underground marijuana culture magazine *THC EXPOSE*, which sadly folded after the second issue.

I arrived on my Jet Blue flight eight hours before the story recital was to begin, and called my wife back home as I sat in the never ending line of taxis heading into Manhattan.

"Hey!" I squealed, filled with anticipation. "This is going to be a great time!"

"Do NOT spend a bunch of money," my wife countered.

"I won't," I said. "Besides, it's all paid for… They're putting me up, there's food and an open bar and everything. Anyways, I can get through a week on like, 30 bucks. I won't spend more than like, 200 dollars."

"Don't go out and buy wine," she cautioned. "That town overcharges for everything… If you need to get drunk, go buy a bottle at a grocery store and drink it in your hotel room."

"Right," I said. "No problem."

The thought of spending an evening in New York City straddling the filthy sheets of a SoHo Radisson with a plastic cup full of Chilean Merlot while watching *SportsCenter* seemed horrendous. After all, I was in "The Big Apple"! "The City That Never Sleeps"! This wasn't the "City Where the Guy Away From His Family For One Night Sits Alone Drinking Wine in his Hotel Room".

By the end of the evening, I was wishing I had followed my wife's advice.

I dropped my first $100 getting into Manhattan. I made the classic New York mistake of getting into a gypsy cab with a driver named "Doopsha" who took me to SoHo and charged me extra because he said the tolls had skyrocketed. Not knowing what to believe, I paid him and walked into my hotel, prepared to decompress for an hour or two before going out to find some food.

The hotel had no record of my reservation. Apparently the hosts of the festival had not booked me like they were supposed to, and I now was being told that I needed to pay $379 for the room, the standard "walk-in price".

Excuse me? *Walk-in price?* What if I had *jogged* in, would it be any cheaper?

The desk clerk was not amused. She ran my credit card as I frantically texted the festival hosts and told them what was happening. I did not hear back. Still, I figured they would cover the expense and reimburse me.

After a long shower, I went through my standard hotel room routine; it starts with the naked stroll in front of the window, followed by the full body shave that leaves hair all over the bathroom floor, and finishes with a half-hour nude television session with my junk pressed up against a cold pillow.

I'm not the only one who does that, right?

After a quick nap, I decided to ride the subway over to the East Village and find the rooftop where the event was scheduled to take place and get comfortable beforehand. I opened my laptop and logged in online, only to be hit with a $14.99 WiFi charge. Unaware that they had free computers in the lobby, and knowing that paying would save me a late night DVD-buying trip to the adult bookstore called "Babeland" that I had passed on the way in, I shrugged it off. (By the way, when I looked up Babeland online, they were offering the following in-store promotion: *Receive 25% off any lube when you purchase a vibrator at any of our stores. Valid until February 14, 2013. Happy Valentine's Day!*)

Down in the lobby, I purchased some toothpaste and a tiny $9.00 bottle of Renu Multi-Purpose eye solution along with the New York Post. Within its pages, I discovered that the previous afternoon a psychotic racist woman had pushed a Middle Eastern man to his death on the subway tracks at the station nearest my hotel. Paranoid that a copycat incident might befall me once I stepped onto the subway platform, I decided to stay above ground, and summoned a taxi instead.

Following the $15.00 ride to the East Village, I stepped into an Italian restaurant to catch the score of the Knicks game, joining a bunch of local fans cursing at the TV. I decided I would buy one glass of wine, knowing that it would probably be my last before going to the event, where the open bar would keep me well-lubricated for the rest of the night. I ordered the house Chianti.

16 bucks.

After downing it in three sips while admiring Carmelo Anthony's offensive output, I cursed myself for ordering the drink and made my way over the venue. It was then that I realized that I was dealing with a faction of complete amateurs. Outside the doorway, a makeshift sign that looked as if it had been printed by some NYU freshman flunking graphic design, read:

"New Poets and Writers Rooftop Rectal"

Yes, RECTAL.

I called attention to it at the door before giving my name to the bouncer, a man way too large and intimidating to be working the guest list at an event for writers and poets, and was greeted with a blank stare. He slipped me my artist pass and a small schedule before telling me that Greg and Blaise, the two hosts of the event, were waiting for me in the "green room" upstairs.

Nice, I thought. Finally, a green room. I was looking forward to rubbing elbows with the elite of the New York literary world while noshing Manhattan catering and some red wine. I climbed those steps, daydreaming of exchanging email addresses with Jonathan Safran Foer as Woody Allen and I discussed the flaws in Soren Kierkegaard's criticisms of idealist intellectuals.

Instead, as I walked into the "green room" (the bus-boy stand of the restaurant in the adjoining room), I was greeted with a frozen vegetable platter, bottles of $1.99 Charles Shaw red wine, and a red-haired doofus named Ricky who handed me a tiny water and told me I "sort of looked like Jason Bateman".

So much for Kierkegaard.

Meanwhile, Greg and Blaise were very young. Like, early 20's.

When I told them I needed to be reimbursed for my hotel room, Blaise said, "We already paid the hotel $129 last month."

I told them there was no reservation when I had arrived. They flipped out and informed me that they would not be able to cover my room charges beyond getting me a check for $129.

There went another $250. I was already way over my $200 limit.

Greg apologized and tried to cheer me up by offering up information about the after party.

"After the event, there's a huge party on my dad's boat," he announced. "Trust me bro, it's killer…we're gonna *throw down*."

I cracked the Charles Shaw. There was only one way I was getting through this.

I read my story to an enthusiastic crowd of roughly 25 people. I followed a young writer who received the most laughs all evening with a banal story about how he thought he saw a mermaid in the East River.

When I asked him if he had ever seen the film *Splash*, he responded with a gruff, "No."

"Netflix it," I told him.

Following the readings, they actually brought out some edamame and hummus to snack on. Starving, I put away nearly three full dishes before folding up my story and preparing to attend the after party on the boat. First, however, Greg and Blaise needed to clean up the event.

"We're gonna be about an hour or two, man," they said.

I looked at my watch; it was 10:30. I forgot that New York City nights don't even start until around midnight. Luckily, I was on West Coast time. I wasn't tired and the buzz from my reading had me primed to hit the Manhattan bar scene for the next few hours, especially if we would end up partying on some guy's father's yacht.

I headed downstairs with some other writers, including a guy who claimed he was about to publish his third novel. We found a place called Farley's on Avenue A, and leaned against the old wooden bar. talking about the pathetic festival we had all just been a part of. The novelist sipped his whiskey before saying, "I'm so sorry you flew out for this, man."

I told him I didn't care. He bought me a glass of wine and we drank to creativity.

It was then that I put my credit card down, which is undoubtedly my most consistent mistake. Once I pass a certain threshold of intoxication, I get extremely generous with the liquor. If you are standing near me at a bar when I am in my cups, I will undoubtedly end up buying you a drink. Or two. Or in this case, four. The novelist and I shared stories of East Coast adventures and I showed him pictures of my kids. We talked writing and sports and for the first time in a while, I felt like a man again. As the drinks flowed, I barely noticed Greg and Blaise come in the door and announce that it was time to head to the after party on the boat. They had a few cute girls with them; the novelist perked up. I swiveled on my chair and texted my wife the following lie:

Got a cab home, don't worry… going to sleep. Event was fun – call you in the morning.

I'm pretty sure I did that so I wouldn't face any unnecessary distractions the rest of the evening. After all, a calm wife is a happy wife; she didn't need to know that I was soon to be popping champagne corks off the bow of a yacht into the Hudson River.

When it came time to split the $15 taxi ride with the novelist, I suddenly became aware that my credit card was still planted at that bar back on Avenue A. Luckily the novelist covered me, and we eventually arrived at a nice brownstone tucked away somewhere back near SoHo. Expecting to end up at the Chelsea Piers or in some Upper West Side marina somewhere, my evening was quickly derailed when I noticed Greg pressing the combination to an electronic lock on a garage door. When it finally lifted, I was thunderstruck.

Greg neglected to mention that his father's boat was *above ground* and parked in a garage.

"Get on, boys!" he yelled. "There should be margarita mix inside!"

I climbed a ladder from the cement floor and did my best to try and stay festive with the party-goers, but for me, this was the final straw. I was still hungry, and unwilling to spend the next four hours listening to some electronic musical dildo like Avicii on the deck of a boat in a dark garage. Concerned about my credit card, I pulled what we like to call an "Irish Goodbye" and quietly slipped out the door with three bottles of water under my arm.

Following a three block walk to a major street, I was able to flag a cab and weave my way back to the bar on Avenue A, convincing the driver I would have money for him at the bar. He cursed at me in Pakistani; I wrote down what he said, hoping to look it up on my laptop when I made it to the hotel.

"Behanchood… Tatti Kaa."

When we arrived, I closed my tab at the bar. Nine drinks and a bag of barbecue Lay's cost me $111.98. At that point, I was so tired I didn't even care. I slayed two $4.25 slices of pizza from the all-night place next door while the meter ran, and eventually made it back to SoHo where the foul-mouthed driver charged me $49.00 for my cross-town detour. I tipped him three dollars and stumbled into the lobby, where I was greeted by a new hotel clerk asking me if I was going to require a late check out.

"Hell yes," I exclaimed.

I also pre-ordered my breakfast, knowing full well that I would not be in the mood to go out searching for egg whites and coffee the next morning. The charge for eggs, coffee, fruit, and room service? $65.00.

That night, after I crawled into bed, I went through my receipts.

In exactly 11 hours and 32 minutes in New York, I managed to spend the following:

Car into Manhattan: $100.00

Hotel Room (after $129 refund) $250.00

Hotel WiFi: $14.99

New York Post/Toiletries in Lobby: $17.50

Cab to East Village: $15.00

Glass of Wine at Italian Restaurant: $16.00

Drinks at 2A Bar on Avenue A: $111.98

Two Slices of Pizza: $8.50

Cab from Soho to East Village to SoHo: $49.00

In Room Breakfast: $65.00

The grand total? $647.97. I could have stayed home and bought myself an iPad Mini.

Before shutting off the TV and climbing under the starched bed sheets, I remembered to look up what the Pakistani taxi driver had said to me in his native tongue. I entered it into a Google search bar and watched as the following popped up:

Behanchood… Tatti Kaa.

Translation? *Sisterfucker… Eat shut.*

I wasn't quite sure what "shut" was, but I had a pretty good idea.

Upon arriving home the next afternoon, I tried to explain to my wife that all of the circumstances were out of my control and that I was miserable the entire time. Unfortunately, this kind of pleading only goes so far and I still ended up looking like a spendthrift loser who squandered a lot of money on absolutely nothing. That night, I promised her it would never happen again.

The following morning, I got an email from Greg and Blaise thanking me for coming and reading at their festival. They said that since it was their first year, they would be making improvements and throwing a kick-ass event the next time. At the end of their email, they invited me back to New York to read any story I liked at the 2014 "New Poets and Writers Rooftop Recital", promising me an incredible opportunity to meet and greet Manhattan's literary community. I responded with one simple phrase.

"Behanchood, Tatti Kaa."

Hopefully, they won't look it up.

I Pledge Allegiance...

Like every sports-loving American father, I am counting on my 3-year-old son to grow up and worship the same teams that I have spent my lifetime following religiously. I can already envision the day he sheds tears when the Arizona Wildcats basketball team wins a Final Four; I see him tailgating with his buddies at USC football games, chugging cans of Iron City Ale when the Steelers take the Super Bowl, and maniacally flipping over a Hyundai Element in a crowded street when the Yankees win a World Series at some point during his lifetime (hopefully avoiding any prison time).

My son already has the countless team-logo onesies, the sippy cups with "Fight On" painted upon their plastic sides, the Derek Jeter batting t-shirt, and a Yankees hat that he never wears. He has an autographed Sean Elliott basketball in his room (mine), a Terrible Towel hanging on his wall, and a Matt Leinart rookie card that I had framed in a protective air-tight case a few years back (I know, a waste of money). Yes, my son is primed to catch on to my loyalties. I want him to share my elation and my heartbreak. I want him to call me twenty years from now when he is in some seedy bar with his friends screaming at some young Arizona Wildcat point guard to "sack up".

I am not alone here; these are the dreams of every young father I meet.

With the current state of sports being what it is, however, I have to look at these possibilities from a realistic point of view and realize that *there is absolutely no way this is going to happen.*

I have been the subject of constant ridicule from my sports-loving friends since I was a child. See, I was born into a desolate sports area. Growing up in Tucson in the early 80's forced kids to find their own favorite teams based on one of three things:

1) The coolest uniforms,

2) The team who won the most games or,

3) The teams your dad liked.

My favorite teams, like many of my friends, were a product of all three.

My dad made it abundantly clear from the minute I could gurgle that I would be growing up a New York Yankees fan. He called me "Little Chambliss" for the entire fall of 1976. Mickey Mantle's name was said around my house more than "I love you", and by the time Reggie Jackson belted those three home runs in the 1978 World Series, I was hooked on the pinstripes.

Then a few years later, my dad attempted to convert his 4-year-old son into a New York Giants fan. This didn't go as well. To this day, my dad wonders how he failed to successfully metamorphose me into a fan of the men in blue. I can now reveal the errors of my father's ways.

I remember when we watched a game on TV, and the their lame helmets came on the screen, printed simply with the word "GIANTS". What was that? I owned about 200 football cards at the time, and I was already aware of the minor-league uniforms the pathetic Giants suited up in every Sunday; I'd be damned if I was going to root for those knobs. The only lamer uniform at the time was that of the Tampa Bay Buccaneers, a pumpkin patch tangerine-colored atrocity. (Although now, the throwback Tampa Bay jersey is one of my favorites in the NFL.)

I had another team in mind. I pulled out the stack of 1980 Topps cards that I had been pining over for weeks, and showed my pops *my* favorite team. JACK HAM. JACK LAMBERT. TERRY BRADSHAW. And the dude with the Bee Gees beard, FRANCO HARRIS.

"The Steelers?" he gasped. "You can't like the Steelers! Like the Giants! Look at this guy, Phil Simms! He's the *future!*"

I looked at Simms. Alright, he had a cannon for an arm, but his name was PHIL SIMMS. I knew three guys at school named Phil. I didn't know anybody with a name as cool as "Franco Harris". Plus, the Steelers wore black and gold. They were MEN. Half the team was missing teeth, and I had no idea what that weird three-starred colorful logo meant, but I loved it. I was sold. The Steelers were cooler.

My dad continued trying to get me to like the Giants, but with each passing week I became a bigger Pittsburgh Steelers superfan. My mom still recalls having to drive to the Sears in town to get me a cheap imitation Jack Lambert jersey a few years later. My dad, who had bought me an "authentic" Lawrence Taylor jersey in 1985, cringed every elementary school picture day when I rolled into the photo session trying to look like I led the Steelers in tackles.

My dad's secret shame was that he couldn't get me to follow his beloved G-Men. And now, raising a son of my own, I have no idea why *any* dad feels as if they'll be able to get their kids to follow their favorite teams, *especially* growing up in Los Angeles. It is nearly impossible.

So I want to weigh the possibility of my son becoming a fan of the exact same teams I live and die for. Here we go…

NEW YORK YANKEES

This has to be the one no-brainer. Even my younger brother, who prefers watching *Top Chef* to the NBA, follows the Yankees. This team has been passed down through five generations of my family. I will know I have failed as a father the day my son comes home with a Dustin Pedroia jersey, saying, "The Sox are just so gritty and tough!"

However, there is a *huge* potential obstacle in my way: THE LOS ANGELES DODGERS. Every guy I know from L.A. loves the Dodgers. They all have season tickets, which I get access to quite a bit, and I do often take my son to Dodgers games; they're quite fun. The weather is beautiful, the fans are great, and Yankee Stadium is 4,000 miles away. This, coupled with a few too many schoolyard arguments amongst his friends, might disrupt 75 years of Selwyn family tradition. So yes, I can see how a few Bat Days and Yasiel Puig autographs might have my son bleeding Dodger blue by his 10th birthday; it's going to be an uphill battle.

Note to self: Get him to Yankee Stadium STAT.

PITTSBURGH STEELERS

There is a chance, albeit a slight one, that my son *might* become a Steelers fan. Why? We live in Los Angeles. No local NFL team, no allegiance! Exactly like me growing up. I've already got him enough Steelers garb to last him well into the 6th or 7th grade. Still, I might find him staring at an old Jamarcus Russell football card in a few years, saying, "Dad! I like these Raiders! I know too many guys named 'Ben Roethlisberger' at school…I don't know anyone named 'Jamarcus'!" If my kid *does* become a Raiders fan, I will absolutely support it, the same way my dad did when he saw me calling Louis Lipps' number instead of Phil McConkey's in a game of Nerf Football on the lawn.

Still, it'll be tough on the heart.

ARIZONA WILDCATS (College Basketball/Baseball)

I will go to the grave with Lute Olsen and Sean Elliott as my two all-time favorite people in sports. Growing up in that barren desert, these guys were my saviors. My ticket out. Winners. My dad and brother and myself WORSHIP the Arizona basketball program, and I cry every time they get knocked out of March Madness. I went to every single home game from 1983 – 1993. Upon arriving at USC, I went to *one* USC home game...the time they played the Wildcats. I sat in the visitor section with my friend Brad, another Tucson Trojan, and we cheered 'Zona's victory the entire time as my chagrined R.A. glared at us from across the nearly empty LA Sports Arena bleachers. That being said, my son might have a good shot at becoming a 'Cats fan…unless he lets UCLA or USC corrupt his young Californian mind; it's going to be tough to compete with all those damn titles in Westwood and all that illegal recruiting at USC.

I guess he might like the 'Cats because I will definitely be taking him to some games with my dad (still a season ticket holder) throughout the years. But once he goes to college I can see him jumping ship, especially since he will *not* be growing up in Tucson.

(Lord, PLEASE let it be anywhere other than Duke.)

USC TROJANS (Football)

The reason I follow USC football and not Arizona football is because, well, I didn't go to a lot of games in Tucson while I was growing up there. I still enjoy the Arizona program, and have fond memories of players like Chuck Cecil - but aside from making out with some girl from Salpointe High School after a loss to Oregon State in 1991 beneath the student section, the 'Cats were never my thing.

And then one semester at USC turned me.

Upon arriving on campus in 1993, Coach John Robinson promised me a national title within four years. Well, we didn't really come close, but we did get a Rose Bowl, Carson Palmer, and Keyshawn Johnson. That national title proved elusive until I was well out of college but still loving USC, despite owing $125,000 in student loans. The official turning point for me was the final game my freshman year, when we threw an interception with a minute left against UCLA.

UCLA went to the Rose Bowl, and we went out drinking.

My friends and I bonded as we drowned our sorrows in enough beer to kill an army; I have been a Trojan faithful ever since. That being said, unless I invest in some season tickets sometime soon, I won't be taking junior to many games during his life. Besides, looking at how easily I was converted to a Trojan football supporter once I arrived on campus, I'm assuming he might bleed his future college's colors someday as well. That will not affect me in any way.

THE NBA (All Of It)

Alright, I know this sucks, but I do not have a favorite NBA team. I have always liked teams that recruited former Arizona Wildcats, so I have rooted for countless teams over the years. If I had to say I *liked* a team, it would be the Phoenix Suns; I fell in love with that Barkley/Ainge/Majerle squad in 1993. But really, I like individual players and different teams year-to-year more than I do one specific team. That being said, my son has full permission to choose whatever team he prefers. Lakers? No problem. I liked them once, too (in the Shaq/Kobe days). Knicks? Why not? They're one of my dad's favorite teams. (My dad failed with me on this one too, although Patrick Ewing was an early childhood favorite.) Wherever Lebron plays? Sure. Love that guy. Personally, I can't think of any choice he might make here that would upset me, other than choosing the WNBA as his favorite professional hoops league. Then we might have to talk.

(As of this pressing, high-flying Lob City hoopsters Blake Griffin and Chris Paul have the Clippers as my son's early favorite team…)

THE NHL, MAJOR LEAGUE SOCCER and ANY OTHER SPORT

I enjoy hockey, soccer, horse racing, badminton, whatever…I just don't *follow* these sports. I love attending NHL games and watching live soccer (especially the World Cup, but I have yet to find an allegiance to a team from most of these sports. My son has free reign to reel me in. If he becomes a huge Phoenix Coyotes fan? Terrific. I will too. Should he begin traveling to see the LA Galaxy battle the Columbus Crew with a bunch of his buddies? I might hitch a ride and buy the beer. Most likely, I will become a fan as well. That is the beauty of sports in America today; we live in a time where you develop your favorite team because you grow up somewhere, or because you enjoyed a highlight you saw 322 times on ESPN one night, or even because your dad beat you up until you agreed with him that one-time Yankees pitcher Phil Coke has "Hall of Fame stuff"…it's all the same.

It's why I like a team from New York, a team from Pittsburgh, and a team from Arizona. It's why my son will undoubtedly place his own loyalties to whatever teams he deems worthy. And whoever he chooses, I will support…

Unless he comes home with that Dustin Pedroia jersey on.

Heisenberg

Upon arriving in southern California in 1993, my first mission was to locate the legendary "chronic" that rapper Dr. Dre had made famous on his classic record of the same name the year before.

Growing up in Tucson, Arizona, I was used to the cheap, dirt brown Mexican grass that came up from Nogales in mashed brick packages. At 100 dollars an ounce, it was affordable and certainly did the trick, but it always left me haggard, unmotivated, and hazy the next morning.

Dr. Dre claimed he never had that hangover. Therefore, I had to find me some *chronic.*

Back then, you could pick up the same dirt weed at 5th and Alvarado in pre-Staples Center downtown Los Angeles. You would drive there in your car and thrust 25 bucks out of your window. Within two minutes, eight weed dealers would be shoving quarter-ounce bags in your hands while offering you fake ID's and "one hour in a hotel with very sexy mujer". We called the place "The Drive Thru".

After suffering from the same malaise and fogginess following our smoke sessions, I decided that what I was buying on the street was actually a grade below my weed from Tucson. It sucked. But I was having no luck trying to locate this mythical chronic; everybody was talking about it, but nobody had it.

And then, I met Tyrone.

Tyrone was a security guard at USC, working the gate just off 45th Avenue and Jefferson Boulevard. At 20, he had been in and out of juvenile hall his entire life and was finally trying to follow the straight and narrow. Of course, he also dealt weed.

"You want chronic, homie?" he asked under his breath when he allowed me to sneak my 1988 Dodge Lancer into the parking garage one Tuesday afternoon. "I got the best shit in town."

How Tyrone knew I smoked weed was a mystery to me. Perhaps it was the Grateful Dead sticker on my bumper or the Cypress Hill booming from my stereo. Or, it could have been the 98 discarded Jack in the Box and Taco Bell wrappers strewn across the floor of my car.

"Really?" I responded in wide-eyed wonder. "Like, THE chronic?"

"Hell yeah, homie, come see me in a minute."

I parked my car and made my way back to Tyrone.

"60 bucks an eighth," he said while slipping me a joint. "This 'J' is for free. Smoke that shit, if you hate it, we never talk again...now get the hell outta my booth."

I pocketed the joint and slipped back towards my dorm room in Pardee Tower. *60 bucks an eighth?* I thought to myself. This guy was out of his mind, obviously trying to rip off a little college freshman with overpriced weed. He was taking advantage of Dr. Dre's boisterous marijuanalogues. I wasn't going to be taken as a sucker.

Nervously, I recruited my friend Matt to come puff the free joint with me. Matt had grown up in Northern California had a long history with Humboldt County herb; he claimed he knew what was real and what was not. We threw on some Dr. Dre, made a odor-masking device out of some Bounce fabric softener and a toilet paper roll, laid a towel beneath the crack of the door, and inhaled.

Within seconds we were on the floor. We spent most of the next two hours pointing at each other and laughing, analyzing the Doors' "Waiting For the Sun" record and talking about how we wished we were "grubbing" Carl's Jr. ("Grubbing" was early 90's slang for "eating" and by far, the lamest term I ever used during my late teens.)

When we came down a few hours later, we were giddy and happy. I had never come down from being high to such an elated state. Normally, I woke up in my clothes, clutching a stuffed animal from my childhood, with a tube sock and an open *Sports Illustrated* swimsuit issue lying next to me. This shit was different.

I truly believed we had found the best stuff I had ever smoked.

After heading to the Sunshine Market to buy some Mickey's 40's and get some cash, we swung by Tyrone's post to inquire about more of the sacred green he had passed my way hours before. Without making eye contact, he told us to give him a dorm room number and to wait for him there. I did, suspiciously, and returned to room 112 to await Tyrone, my drug dealing security guard.

Roughly two hours passed.

I tried to work on a Comp 101 paper, but had nothing. My Spanish homework looked like German to me. The only thing that was remotely interesting was a rerun of *Family Matters* on TV. This education was costing 25,000 dollars a year…my parents would be so proud.

Finally, Tyrone knocked and we let him in. He broke down his weed system like a street hustler unloading stereo equipment. It was fascinating to watch.

"Y'all want joints, they're 10 bucks apiece. Eighths are 60, Ounces 480 and QP's…well, y'all don't look like you ready for a QP just yet."

Matt and I decided on an eighth, meaning 30 bucks a man. I had a 20 dollar bill and so did Neil. We had two options: we could either include Scott Stokes from across the hall, a notorious weed moocher, or I could dip into my wallet and spend my "Emergency 20".

Let me back up. My grandmother gave me a twenty dollar bill the day I packed my bags for college. She had given my mother an emergency twenty herself way back in 1964 and my mom had *kept the same bill for thirty years.* It was a symbol of family and love and parental guidance and trust. I will always remember her heartfelt and sincere words of advice as she handed over that twenty dollar bill.

"Zach, this is an "Emergency 20". This is only to be used in an absolute *EMERGENCY*, okay?"

I nodded yes and kissed my grandma goodbye. I had truly intended to respect her wishes and hold on to that keepsake for my entire life. But, here I was, three weeks into college, faced with a dilemma. We were twenty dollars short, and I had a twenty dollar bill hidden in my wallet. I looked at Matt. He looked at Tyrone. We all looked at each other. Minutes passed.

"Well, this *is* an emergency!" I rationalized.

Within three minutes the deal had gone down, Tyrone sped off in his souped-up VW Bug, and Matt and I passed joints around for the next three hours. Sorry, Grandma.

As the months passed and I found myself broke, I returned to Tucson for Thanksgiving, intent on spreading the word about the sticky green "kind bud" that was circulating around Los Angeles. I flew home with a small sample of the stuff, and impressed my friends with late-night smoke sessions that led to insane laughter, brilliant creativity, and dozens of screenings of *Up in Smoke.*

Nintendo hockey led to midnight swimming, which led to occasional girls stopping by. We took my fried Greg's car out after two a.m. just to drive around empty streets. We felt like true O.G.'s bumping "Nuthin' But a G Thang" out of the windows as we rolled five deep into a fast food parking lot. It was all so daring and adventurous at the time. Now it just seems like childish nonsense, but at the time it was *livin'.*

It was around winter break back in Tucson when my friend Greg came upon a strain of Tucson marijuana that looked green, fluffy, and delicious, but gave you the same high as a bag of dirty Mexican schwag. It was deceptively tasty, but it wasn't the best high ever. Still, it did the trick and, best of all only cost 25 dollars a quarter.

An idea was hatched.

"If I bought an ounce of this at 100 bucks, I could sell it in my dorm for 60 bucks an eighth to these naïve USC kids who think it's chronic!" I suggested.

Greg, ever willing to make a buck, raised an eyebrow. "Dude, if we throw orange peels in it, it'll give it some danky smell and nobody will know the difference."

I smiled at him. What a great idea.

Greg continued, "I'll buy some tomorrow, we'll package it as twenty bags and make $380!"

And just like that, my drug running days had begun. It was going to be so easy: buy the ounce in Tucson, fly it carefully to LA, and unload it at a rapid pace from my dorm room. If anything, it would get me a little spending cash; to an 18-year-old kid, $320 dollars is a lot of money.

I mean, what were my expenses?

Condoms (which I never had a chance to use).

Beer (two dollars a 40 ounce at the local Korean market).

McDonald's ($2.99 for the Big Mac extra value meal).

And rap, Phish, and Doors CD's.

Weed was another definite must-have. So, as long as I didn't get high on my own supply, I would have enough to support my minor pot habit.

The deal was set. Greg laid out the seed money (so to speak) and I became the desert weed liaison to the college dorm scene at the University of Southern California. I loaded up a cargo jacket with about twenty mini bags of orange-scented grass and got on Southwest flight number 132 to Los Angeles.

Nervous as hell, I successfully passed through the same security checkpoint that Arizona superstar basketball player Damon Stoudamire would get caught transporting marijuana through five years later. When I landed in LA, my roommate picked me up and within an hour down the 105 freeway, I had cracked one of the bags and packed my buddy's pipe with a "sample" of the goods.

So much for not getting high on my own supply.

"It's a celebration bowl," I declared. "I'll pay for that one out of my own pocket."

We got stoned, laughed all the way home and spent the night demolishing three of the bags in the cache.

Thus began the horrible pilfering of my own marijuana. If Greg had been more like Gustavo Fring from *Breaking Bad*, I would have been beheaded by now. Still, I somehow believed I was about to make a lot of money.

Kara Sherman was a tall freshman from Cincinnati in the Theta sorority who enjoyed Janet Jackson and getting stoned; she quickly became my first victim. When she heard I had "bags" for sale, she entered my dorm room and bought forty dollars worth after we discussed how awesome "That's the Way Love Goes" from Janet's new CD was. Insinuating that I was in possession of some serious crazy herb, I told her to tell her friends about me and spread the love.

Within days, the entire freshman Theta sorority rush class, along with some first-time stoners, had come through my doors. Women were easier targets because one got the sense that they were smoking for the first time, trying to show the guys they were dating that they had an adventurous side.

Kara's friend Lara bought a bag.

So did Julie Cullum, who also stuck around to make out with me after we smoked. I felt like that cool dude who deals pot and dates Milla Jovovich in *Dazed and Confused.* My hair was getting longer, I was playing guitar, and life was moving along…

I was getting a "cute pot dealer" label from the young sorority women, and I loved it. It was outlaw. Kara Sherman came by weekly, and one night after we had kissed she invited me to the Theta "invite dance" set to take place in a month. I had suddenly become much cooler. I had a date to a dance with a hot chick, and was getting respect from upperclassmen and gorgeous California girls.

I thought things were going to be alright in this drug game…that was, until Joe Davidson stopped by to check out my stash.

Joe Davidson was a laid-back California native who wore flip-flops, Reyn Spooner shirts and surf shorts every day. Even in the winter. His marijuana intake was herculean, as was his affinity for booze and other drugs; we had become acquainted through a joint passed during freshman orientation the summer before. He was a slow-drawled Orange County legend who, it was said, got a DUI at 18 and entertained a different gorgeous woman in his bed nightly. He also ran a small business out of his dorm room. He rented VHS tapes of pornography to horny guys in the fraternity system (this was waaay before the internet, my friend). Finally, it was rumored that he was awaiting some five million dollar trust fund should he make it to his 22nd birthday.

He had heard I was "holding", and made his way into my room just as I had sold a Pi Phi girl named Christine a small bag of weed and let her borrow an Enya CD.

"Sup, dude, I heard you've got buds," he said.

"Yeah, man, buds so kind they say 'please' and 'thank you'," I said, channeling the voice I imagined a surfer-friendly drug dealer would have. Joe laughed.

The main thing I learned during my time as a pot dealer was to study your buyers carefully, and then create an alternate persona to relate to their interests. I was a master of this improvisational game; it's how I convinced Kara Sherman I loved Janet Jackson. I *knew* my clients, and I knew how to bullshit. If a prospective buyer began talking about throwing pottery, I'd begin talking about how much more accurate ceramic kilns were than rotary ones. If a prospective buyer enjoyed talking about the best ways to make tamales, by God, I would enter into that conversation as if I was running a Mexican food truck outside of a construction site.

In this case, Joe Davidson's main interest was weed.

I showed him the bag. He smelled it. He examined it. He broke it down as if he were a judge at the Cannabis Cup. Had he spent this much effort on his school work, he would have been USC's valedic-fucking-torian.

Then, he LAUGHED.

"Dude, you're scamming everybody," he said.

"Huh?" I asked, playing dumb.

"This is low-grade Mexi-schwag. You probably got it down on 5th and Alvarado and threw orange peels in it for a week to give it some danky smell."

I pretended to have no idea what he was talking about.

"C'mon dude – I know your game…ripping off sorority chicks and amateur puffers on this bullshit just because you know the difference between kind bud and schwag… you're a criminal dude!"

I was called out and humiliated.

"Wanna listen to 'Waiting for the Sun'?" I asked.

Joe gave me five dollars for a small bag, stating that he would pay what the weed was worth. He then proceeded to pack the buds into my mini bong decorated with mysterious Chinese symbols, which we had named "Bong Duck Dong" one night while stoned and watching *Sixteen Candles*.

Joe smiled and exhaled.

"Yup, Mexican schwag disguised as kind bud…If I didn't do the same shit all throughout high school, I'd rat you out," he exclaimed.

I took a puff after him and contemplated my position.

"Dude, don't say anything, OK? I got a good scam here…"

"Hahah, dude… I ain't like that. Just give me three more bags so it's like a 20 dollar quarter."

Called out and somewhat intimidated by this real-life Jeff Spicoli, so much cooler than me with my Brandon Walsh sideburns and haircut, I caved. Joe Davidson walked out of my room with a quarter-ounce of my weed for 25 bucks, and just like that, I was down to my last few bags.

"I'm quitting the drug game," I told Greg over the phone.

"What, man?" he said. "How much money have we made?"

I looked at the supply. In my dorm room safe, I had $220, a far cry from the $380 we were hoping to make. Plus, Greg had laid out 100 bucks to buy the first ounce, so after paying him back…I would walk away with 60 dollars.

60 freaking dollars!

I had illegally transported weed across state lines. I had sold it to unsuspecting strangers. I developed a reputation as a pot dealer and had embarrassed myself in front of Joe Davidson. I could have gone to jail for five years. In fact, the best thing to come out of the whole situation was a date with Kara and a make out session with Julie Cullum.

"I want out," I told him again. "I got ambushed. People found out about our scam and we're both going to make about 60 bucks."

Greg wasn't happy, and blamed me for smoking the entire supply. In reality, I had only dug into about 100 bucks worth, but he didn't need to know that. He chastised me like Walter White to Jesse Pinkman.

"Sell those last three bags and redeem yourself. Next time we do it my way."

Fully knowing that there would not be a next time, I decided to unload the final three bags and retire from the game, "One Last Score". I was going to quit dealing and maybe get a real job, like my friend Brice at the bookstore.

$5.25 an hour.

Kara Sherman was my main mark, so when she came by the dorm for her weekly purchase, I assumed she would be an easy sale.

"Wow, did you see the video for 'If I Was Your Girl' by Janet Jackson?" I started out. "It was awesome; we should get tickets to her show at the Forum."

Kara did not seem amused.

"Zach, I want my money back…"

It quickly dawned on me that Joe Davidson had squealed.

After explaining to her that Joe was wrong and that the weed was actually high quality, she told me that unless I gave her money back and/or the rest of my supply, she would take matters to the USC administration.

I was being blackmailed by a sorority girl.

Kara not only got 45 of her 60 dollars back, but she disinvited me to her formal dance as well. As she left my room calling me a "tool", I yelled out to her across the hall, "Janet Jackson sucks my ASS!"

She huffed and stormed off. I knocked on Matt's door and we finished the final three bags within the next week.

When the smoke had cleared, I had made fifteen bucks and had a lot of angry women talking trash about me. Worst of all, Greg couldn't trust me to be his liaison anymore. It was like *Friday*, and I was Smokey to Greg's Big Worm.

I retired from pot dealing and applied for a job at the bookstore. Within three hours of work, I had guaranteed more money than my entire drug operation had provided me, and I knew that a straight and narrow path was the way to go. However, within a week I was caught smoking a joint in the bathroom by the manager and fired.

A year later I discovered DJ-ing, managing to find a job where I could drink and smoke *during* work while making as much money as any college kid I knew. It was a great gig, and one I spent nearly nine years of my life doing.

As I look back, I wonder if the kids in college now will ever have to deal with not having weed again. Will they ever have to confront a weed dealer? I doubt it. Since the California Caregivers pretty much guarantee that anybody with "terrible migraine headaches" can saunter into a doctor's office and get a medical marijuana card, the days of struggling to access marijuana are over. Pot is suddenly EVERYWHERE; all you need is the card.

Tyrone is out of business at the security gate.

5th and Alvarado dealers are focusing on fake ID's.

And low-rung college freshman are not getting away with easy scams on unsuspecting Midwestern girls with dad's money to burn.

My grandmother is now 90-years-old. She still lives in Tucson, and has absolutely no idea that I spent her emergency twenty on a bag of weed the second month I was in college. As far as she knows, I still keep it in my wallet, the same way my mother has since 1964.

When the time comes to send my son off to college, I hope my mother will give him an emergency twenty as well, and inform him that it is to only be used in a dire situation. I look forward to watching my son accept the cash and pocket it, intending to savor it for his entire life the way he thinks his dad did with his. I look forward to watching him take his grandma's advice and nod his head before hugging her. I look forward to seeing him make a promise he intends to keep…

And then watch him speed off to the medical marijuana store to relieve his newly-diagnosed migraine headache.

The Letter

The very fact that anybody is even reading this collection of stories right now amazes me, and I feel inclined to share with you a letter given to me by my creative writing professor when I attended the University of Southern California in the spring of 1997. Having spent four years writing (somewhat) funny, first person accounts of college life, I had come to believe that my storytelling ability would someday lead to a Woody Allen- or Steve Martin-esque screenwriting career, allowing me to publish stories in periodicals like *The New Yorker* whenever I pleased.

I was aware that my fiction, with titles like "Walk of Shame", "Drinking and Dialing", and "How to Get Drunk on Three Dollars at a College Bar", garnered me my first group of college fans; I also knew these pieces left most adult readers wondering what had gone wrong with the children of the baby-boomer generation. To be honest, my parents weren't exactly fans.

I was not a revolutionary. I was certainly no political protestor. I was simply a self-proclaimed humorist who loved to write columns about terrible one-night stands and sorority girl hand-jobs. Had I pursued my writing career with the necessary fervor of anyone dreaming of a life in print, I would have most likely ended up writing for the "lad mags" of the late 90's like *Maxim, FHM,* or *Stuff.* Instead, I began writing sketch comedy and screenplays, and soon ended up on a TV show penned by all the *former* writers of those magazines. So oddly enough, it all came full circle. But back when I was a senior in college, I contended with a creative writing professor who was a thrice-published and *New York Times* Best Selling author, who greeted every story I turned with with exasperation. Possibly because I was writing stories titled "Bong Construction in the Dorm Room".

Which leads me back to this letter.

Professor Don Markert was a teetotaling, tweed coat wearing man with a strange tendency to eat bowls of cereal in the middle of class discussions. He ate about two bowls a class; from what I gathered, he always ate some sort of imitation Cheerios, which only made him seem stuffier and more pretentious. Mr. Markert's favorite writers were Hemingway and Charles Dickens; I barely registered even a snicker when, after going around to each student and asking them who their favorite writers were, I jokingly replied, "the legendary John Grisham."

Markert looked down on Bukowski ("a 3rd rate drunken poet"), Kerouac ("a speed freak with no punctuation"), and even my secret airplane obsession, Louis L'Amour ("wasn't even from the West").

His mind seemed so limited at times, the fact that he was teaching a creative writing class made us all uncomfortable. But I still believed that I could charm my way into his good graces when I submitted my final piece to him. I had rewritten it five times, and even delivered it clad in a plastic folder I had splurged an extra $1.25 on to make it look more professional and staple-free.

A week earlier, I had actually published the story about bong construction in the local fraternity-friendly rag *28th Street Magazine* – and along the Greek houses of fraternity row, it was a hit. People stopped me at bars every night and told me how much they loved my stories, the "Bong Story" being a particular favorite amongst the masses.

When I turned it in as my final college short story, I was anxiously awaiting some gracious recognition for my originality. After all, other kids had written their final stories on their tap-dancing grandmothers, or the harrowing time when their lifelong family dog died; to me, it all just seemed so lame. In my mind, I was the only student taking a risk. I wrote a story about how my roommate and I impressed our dates by fabricating a bong out of a dorm friend's asthma inhaler, two toilet papers rolls, and some tin foil. We all listened to Snoop Dogg and made out for hours. I expected nothing less than an A plus.

Mr. Markert summoned me to his office the following Thursday for our final conference before I was to graduate. He was going to critique my story and then offer me some advice. I went in confident.

"Zach, sit down," he said, pouring a bowl of cereal from a bag that read *Honey Nut Scooters*. Back before Google, it took me a week to figure out these were a generic 99 Cent Store cereal brand that "simulated the taste of Honey Nut Cheerios". I scoffed at the absurdity of a grown man eating bagged cereal at four o'clock in the afternoon, but then realized that shit, cereal is pretty darn good.

I sat down and refused his offer of a cup of staff lounge coffee, strange considering the amount of coffee I consume now, and prayed that he was going to tell me some publisher had read my collection of stories and was dying to market me as a new voice in American literature. At that moment, the working title of my first book was simply, *College*.

Professor Markert and I talked at length about why I had taken his class. He claimed that my biggest problem as a writer was that my storytelling had not improved in the three months I was his student. He referenced other classmates who wrote from their own unique experiences, like Sean Holden, who had chronicled his miserable life as a USC male cheerleader. Sean's story had even published in the *Orange County Register* the previous month, and his book deal was being negotiated. I was insanely jealous, but I knew I couldn't write a story about male cheerleading. (Sean Holden is now a freelance graphic designer. His book was never greenlit.)

Stating that I didn't have any cheerleading experience, Mr. Markert asked me what exactly I had been doing for four years in college, to which I replied, "Drinking, drugs, playing music, acting, writing, going to concerts, having sex, laughing and convincing my parents that I was learning something."

He frowned and said, "Well, no wonder your stories are so self-obsessed."

Mr. Market then handed me my final letter of opinion, stating he hoped it would be something I looked back upon in the future and thanked him for. He told me not to open it until I got home, and that everything in the letter was his true, honest, and forthright opinion. He informed me I would be receiving a B minus in the class, which seemed low to me; we shook hands and said goodbye, avoiding any eye contact. I managed to mutter the word "dick" under my breath as I stepped out of his office for the last time.

When I got back to my apartment, I cracked a beer and collapsed on the couch, where my undoubtedly stoned roommate Simon sat watching a rerun of the *X-Files*. I opened the manila envelope. Here is exactly what Mr. Markert's letter said:

"*Dearest Zack,*

Throughout this semester, I have been continually appalled by your attempts at constructing anything slightly above what a horny midwestern teenager might find amusing. Your sophomoric humor and lack of wit is apparent everywhere and although you claim to have been writing since you were a boy, your sloppy vocabulary, ridiculous thought patterns and poor word and subject structure make you quite possibly the most embarrassing student I have had in this class in nearly three years. Should you continue to pursue a career as a fiction writer, you must understand that you need to read more and stop directing your attention upon your self-centered accolades. You write of girls and keg-stands and marijuana the way a backwoods hunter writes of shooting a twelve-point buck... But let me tell you, Mr. Selwyn, you are not the first person in the world to drink a beer, smoke a marijuana cigarette or hump a Tri-Delt. In fact, you might be 60 years beyond the respectable alternative writers that you consider your peers and equals. Right now you remind me of the kid who moons me from the back of the school bus – far from a young man who will graduate from the University of Southern California with a journalism degree and expect to get a writing job anywhere but in your own pathetic journal entries. My final advice to you is to get into real estate or law. Some profession where you can sell your bullshit anywhere other than on the written page. No magazine will ever publish you - and I say this as a professor of creative fiction writing. Should you continue to pursue this career you claim you want so badly, I wish you the best of luck and can only advise you that the homeless shelter on Flower Street has a very nice daily boxed lunch."

Woah. Adding insult to injury, he had spelled *my fucking name wrong*!

I read the letter to Simon, who did his best to control his hysterical laughter. He couldn't believe the level of hatred my professor had spewed forth in his final letter. At the very end, after repeating the line in which my professor stated I would end up a homeless comedy writer, I joined Simon in lighting a joint and then sank into my couch, depressed. Simon did his best to cheer me up.

"Fuck it, I like your stories," he said. "Want some taquitos?"

Graduation. Moving time. Hollywood apartment. $400 / month. I cashed in my bonds and graduation checks to follow my dreams of creative writing and acting and music; by July, I had spent over $1,000 sending out stories to magazines and book publishers only to be greeted with rejection letter after rejection letter. One book publisher encouraged me to keep going with my character, but most of them said, "Not for us." "Doesn't fit with our format." "Sorry, you have a lot of growing to do."

Was Mr. Markert right?

Come fall, I had basically donated my entire life savings to Kinko's and the United States Post Office. All I had to show for it was a pile of rejections and a pack-a-day cigarette habit that was getting worse as I stressed out about my lack of funds and prospects. Around August, I was down to my last few dollars. I was 22-years-old and a month behind on rent. I was out of food and not sure where to turn to next. I decided to sell some CDs.

Back in 1997, selling twenty CD's meant earning roughly $50 cash at the Heavy Rotation record store in the Valley. (Nowadays, that's roughly $3 in trade at the famous Amoeba Records in Hollywood.)

Knowing I had to make fifty bucks last as long as I could, I decided to hit the grocery store and stock up on dry and canned foods that might last me until some more money came in. As I cased the aisles for clearance items, it suddenly dawned on me that buying cereal for $3.99 was a huge mistake. Within minutes I was at the 99 Cent store, stocking up on bags of, yep, *Honey Nut Scooters.*

At first I was embarrassed. But then I realized something; if Mr. Markert was so successful, why was *he* eating food from the 99 Cent store? Shouldn't a thrice-published "writing expert" at least enjoy boxed cereal once in awhile? Who was *he* to say I would end up failing? In reality, all he was doing was disparaging young minds, preventing them from becoming as successful as they could. Oh my God, I thought. Did Mr. Markert see me as a *threat*?

That afternoon, I went home and wrote a story called "50 Bucks Away From Being Homeless". It flowed and made sense and every phrase and moment felt natural and easy. As the words continued to fill up my laptop screen, I suddenly decided to tell Mr. Markert to shove his career advice up his rear end. I couldn't stop writing because one guy had written me off! If I was able to have experiences that shaped me as a man, I would always write about them, no matter what my professor had told me.

I finished my story the next day and sent it to ten different places: six magazines, three quarterly story collections...and one Mr. Markert, care of the University of Southern California English Department.

The $50 was depleted, but this time I didn't care. I had written something with some meaning and life. A new fire was lit beneath me that I was convinced would carry me to the top of the literary echelon. I felt reborn.

About a month later, the usual rejection letters began piling up.

"You're growing as a writer, but this is not for us..."

"Interesting. We wish you the best but we can't use this right now."

"Thank you for your story, but our magazine is folding."

Even though I failed to sell that story, the rejection letters were at least getting more encouraging. It's like when a girl awkwardly kisses you – but then says she just wants to be friends; at least you got that kiss.

One final letter arrived at my house on a Friday, just as I was going out to begin a new job as a Bar Mitzvah DJ. It was kind and encouraging and not at all what I would have expected. It read as follows:

"*Dearest Zack,*

I am so thrilled to have read your latest short story. It is by far the most mature and engaging piece you have written. To be honest, I never thought you would continue writing after school ended, but you have proven me wrong with your funny and witty piece about my words nearly driving you to Skid Row. I am so impressed by this piece, I would like for you to possibly come share it with my class this upcoming semester. I can even forward it over to a few friends of mine who work in publishing. I like your angle... Young men are supposed to struggle through life. Otherwise, it's never interesting. When you wrote about beer and weed and sex, you came across as pompous and thick-headed. This shows a vulnerability that you have never been willing to share before. Well done.

Your friend,

Mr. Markert"

I folded up his letter, took a deep breath, and went off to work.

For the first time in my life, I truly felt like a successful writer.

Stuck

Every father knows there will come a moment in his life when he will be forced to stand up for his child; whether it's the first time one has to confront a school bully, or the time one finds himself begging a judge to excuse a breaking and entering charge, all men know they will someday have to play rightful guardian.

Trouble finds some kids early. Others seem to flirt with it in junior high or high school. In fact, *my* father had to go to bat for me after some buddies and I were caught stealing a golf cart from the Cleveland Indians Spring Training bullpen in 1992. Luckily, the judge handling our case, Judge Greenfeld, happened to be one of my father's patients. After haggling down the charge from "grand theft golf cart" to simple "teenage tomfoolery", we all walked. My punishment was that I couldn't go see U2 in Phoenix that summer. Judge Greenfeld's reward was free flu shots for life.

I knew that my day too would come. I just figured it would happen in fifteen years or so, when my kids were caught sipping beer in high school or something. Instead, I recently found myself going toe-to-toe in a parking lot with an incensed real estate agent after my pre-pre-pre-adolescent daughter innocently stuck a Trader Joe's sticker on the back of his brand new 2014 Porsche Panamera.

Trader Joe's is my favorite grocery store. In addition to the low prices, they are always generous to my children and offer them lollipops when we come in – as well as rolls of free circular seasonal stickers. The theme of the stickers change about five times a year: Halloween, Thanksgiving, a big one at Christmas, a scratch-and-sniff flower roll for springtime, and finally a panel showcasing whimsical summertime celebrations.

This particular roll that caused all this damage was from the summer collection. The specific sticker in question, held a drawing of a spatula beneath the words "Dressed to Grill."

More often than not, the decals end up on my kids' t-shirts, on top of their hands, and ultimately on the floor of my backseat. For some reason on this day, my daughter decided that the $85,000 dollar car next to us in the parking lot needed a new bumper sticker.

I wasn't aware that she had put the thing on the car until an extremely livid 30-something man yelled at me from the other side of the parking lot:

"What the fuck did that girl put on my car?"

My 7-year-old son's eyes lit up. My daughter pointed at the sticker and giggled. I was aghast at his language in front of my kids.

"Hey man, watch your mouth, would ya?"

"Your fucking daughter just stuck something on my new car, asshole," he responded.

That's then I first noticed what she had done. Sure enough, stuck just to the right of the guy's license plate was a small circular sticker.

The one reading "Dressed to Grill".

"Oh wow," I said, chuckling embarrassedly. "Sorry about that."

"What's so funny?" he yelled. "I'm gonna kick your ass if you don't pay for my car to be detailed."

"Woah, wait, what? Are you kidding me?"

He came around the side of the car and proceeded to bump into me. And not softly, either. The guy wanted to fight me.

"Dude, chill," I said. He didn't chill. Nor did he back down. In fact, this worked-up, roid-raged a-hole was fucking serious. He opened his car door and rifled through a leather briefcase, taking out what looked to be some sort of stick. I got scared. Then, I picked up my daughter and put her in my car. I got my boy inside too.

"Buckle your seatbelt, please."

"What's going on?" he asked, fumbling with the strap.

"Daddy might have to kick somebody's ass."

I have no idea why I said that to my son. I am not a fighter. Never have been. I once scraped the scab off Greg Renner's knee during a scrap on a soccer field and he bled so badly that I was declared the winner, but most of my junior high and high school fights had been resolved by pussy-footing away or by using some sort of sarcastic humor. The last time I was even close to getting into a fight was when a stranger heckled my denim-on-denim ensemble one night after leaving a G. Love and Special Sauce concert at the El Rey Theater. Panicked, I ducked into my friend's car and drove away with my head down, fighting back tears. I think I even began crying, asking my friend, "Why do people have to be so *mean*?"

Basically, I have always been a huge pussy.

"Use your ninja skills, daddy!" my son called out to me. I closed up the car and prepared to do my best to not get humiliated. The guy approached me.

"Look man, why don't you let me just try to get the sticker off with my hands?"

He reached for something in his back pocket and I froze, waiting for a blade or a gun to appear. I was sure I was about to get shanked in front of my children because my three-year-old girl decided that a Porsche was more fun than her Hello Kitty sticker book.

Instead, he pulled out an iPad Mini.

"Donovan's Detail, Hollywood," he said. "175 bucks for a sports cars… you're paying for it."

"Bullshit!" I responded. "Look dude, my daughter is three, okay?"

"You should've been watching her."

"I was, dickface…now let's try and take the sticker off before we overreact here."

"Fuck you, I want my car detailed," he said.

"Or what, man? Are you gonna kick my ass in the Trader Joe's parking lot in front of my kids?"

He looked in my car window and saw their two little heads peering out at the action. I hoped to God that the dude had a heart and would just take the sticker off and drive away. Nope. He stared me down, nostrils flaring.

"I'm calling the cops."

He practically stabbed me with me his insurance information and his business card – "Miller McKay, Real Estate Agent". The worst was the tagline; below a professional headshot were the words *"Miller McKay Moves Million-Dollar Mansions"*.

Miller was handsome, but in that cheesy actor-turned-real-estate-agent way, where you weren't sure if he was gay or not. His teeth had been capped, his hair colored, and his skin artificially tanned. And he drove a Porsche Panamera. In the moment, I remembered Howard Stern's observation: "You drive a Porsche, you're pretty much a douche." On the way into a Porsche dealership, there should be a giant sign reading, "*You're here because you have a small penis.*"

And here was the king cornichon. He forced me to stick around until the cops arrived in the Hollywood Trader Joe's parking lot. By the time they finally arrived, roughly an hour and a half after the incident, I had expected this nonsense to blow over.

"Yeah, we do a full inspection of the vehicle and and make a judgment based on the level of vandalism we assess," the officer told me, cleaning his eyeglasses.

Nervously, I searched for potential charges on my phone, which turned out to be a worse idea than checking WebMD for an inexplicable rash.

In California, vandalism charges are pretty serious. A conviction can result in penalties that include jail time and very large fines. As the guardian of my three-year-old, I would be responsible for her sentence.

One of the major vandalism charges in California is "keying" a car, a crime I myself was victim to when Rachel Fox put a gash in my 1988 Dodge Lancer in the high school parking lot after I told everybody that she kissed like a drunk camel. (I didn't press charges.) Other charges, like writing your name in wet cement or simple wall graffiti, are more serious depending on the value of the damage. According to "Misdemeanor vandalism under Penal Code 594 PC", if damage is *under* $400, it becomes a misdemeanor and you could face any of the following vandalism penalties:

1. Up to one (1) year in a county jail.
2. A maximum fine of one thousand dollars ($1,000)... OR up to five thousand dollars ($5,000) if you have a prior vandalism conviction. (Aside from destroying a few Lego sets, I was pretty sure my daughter had a clean record.)
3. Required counseling. (Maybe not a terrible idea for a three-year-old.)
4. Community service (which may include personally cleaning, repairing, or replacing the damaged property), and/or.

5. Being tasked with keeping the damaged property or another property in the community "graffiti free" – or in this case "sticker free" for up to one year.

Oh God, none of this was good.

The cops analyzed the area of the car where the sticker had been slapped. They carefully removed it and investigated the scene like actors on *CSI: Miami* looking into a murder. It was torturous. Then they spoke with McKay at length, silently pointing back towards my family in the car. I was dying to know what they were talking about. My palms sweat. My head tingled. I flipped on a DVD in the back for the kids as I secretly imagined picking up trash on the side of the highway for the rest of the summer.

I definitely did not feel "Dressed to Grill".

Miller began gesticulating wildy and screaming at the cops. He opened his car door and he got in, grabbing his phone and frantically dialing somebody. A minute later, the two officers came over to my window, and tapped their batons on it for me to roll it down. A lump filled my throat and I did as instructed.

"Did you know this gentleman before this afternoon?" the officer asked.

"No sir. My three-year-old stuck the sticker on his car as we were unloading the bags of groceries."

She smiled at the cop, who nodded his head.

"Well, Mr. Selwyn, here's the deal…"

He paused for a moment and looked back over his shoulder at Miller McKay.

"This guy is in a fantasy world. We don't see any permanent damage. The nice thing for you to do would be to offer Mr. McKay a car wash; nothing too fancy, maybe a ten-dollar hand wash or something like that. But otherwise, this was a waste of time and we're not even going to file a report."

"Seriously? I have to pay for his car to be washed?" I asked.

"Only if you feel inclined. There is no law saying you have to do so, so if not, sir, you are free to go."

I looked into the officer's eyes and smiled. That was that. For once, the dad in the 2005 Lemon Law Subaru Legacy wagon had defeated the hyper-tanned slickster in the Panamera. This was a victory for fathers everywhere, and I rightfully thanked the cop and looked back at my kids, who were actually not watching the DVD, but listening to our exchange with real concern.

"Tell Miller McKay to shove his car wash up his ass," I said.

They smiled. I rolled up the window and drove out to the edge of the parking lot. As I slipped my parking ticket into the machine, it alerted me that my extra hour plus in the lot had rung up a charge of $1.50. A total scam, but at that moment I didn't really care. It was worth it. I had stood up for my children and won. Even better than that was hearing my son tell my wife later, "Daddy almost went *Real Steel* on the guy, mommy!"

"Of course I did," I said.

A lie? Maybe not. Maybe I *would* have kicked Miller McKay's ass if I was forced to. Who knows? Whatever the case, I felt better and stronger with my victory. I cracked a beer, lit the grill and thought, *Bring it on Summer... Bring. It. On.*

MUSEUM OF YOUTH

It has been nearly nineteen years since I left my childhood home for college. In that time, the closet in my old bedroom has been housing the rotting souvenirs of my fading youth, items that will forever sentimentally call out to me from the 1980's. Made invaluable through sentiment, I have been unable to part with these trinkets since I was 13 years old.

Of course, I am referring to thousands of ridiculously worthless *Pac-Man* keychains, Garbage Pail Kids and armless G.I. Joe figures. GoBots and *Star Wars* spaceships are shoved into back drawers next to a myriad of autographed baseballs, ranging from superstars like Gary Sheffield to busts like onetime Cleveland Indians prospect Luis Medina. There are at least 120 baseball-themed posters, like the Jose Canseco-Mark McGwire "Bash Brothers" print and the "Bo Knows Bo" Nike series. And finally, a colossal amount of baseball cards litters the back wall of my closet, long ignored and cast aside.

From what I remember, there is even a small collection of stuffed animals that somehow found themselves packed into a moldy cedar trunk, not unlike the toys Andy from *Toy Story 3* forgot when he eventually headed off to college.

Forgotten and lonely, these items pray that someday their owner will return home and rediscover them, bringing them out for one last playdate…

As I mentioned, the majority of the closet was stuffed with my once extensive collection of baseball memorabilia; I can't deny that I sort of hoped it would remain in that closet forever.

Now, my mother repeatedly told me nightmare stories of her mom accidentally throwing away all of her toys and collectibles when she went off to the University of Wisconsin in 1964. She never forgave her parents for tossing out scores of Mickey Mantle baseball cards and rare *Howdy Doody* collectibles, which were now worth thousands of dollars. So, in my early years, she encouraged me to save items for potential future profits; I jumped into my collecting with a furious passion.

Back then it was cool to own 123,000 baseball cards.

Today, they call it *hoarding*.

My closet has lain virtually dormant for 19 years. In that time, a certain online website known as eBay has shattered the dreams of memorabilia collectors everywhere by revealing that there were a lot more Mike Schmidt rookie baseball cards in the world than we once would have thought. Topps Nolan Ryan rookie cards, previously listed by the *Beckett Baseball Card Monthly* as being worth $725, are now available online for eight bucks. And the holy grail of all kid collectors nationwide, the $100 Don Mattingly 1984 Donruss rookie card, is suddenly available for $14.99.

Even the crown jewel of my collection, my grandfather's 1920-21 Christy Mathewson W514 Strip Card, which an admiring middle-aged man had once tried to trade me a *car* for, is now selling for $250 online…or best offer.

The goldmine in my closet is now officially silt.

The dreaded call finally came from my mother; it was time I went home to clean out my closet of all my old childhood memorabilia. She was turning my room into an office.

"What?" I said. "Clean out my *museum*?"

"If it's a museum, nobody is taking the tour," my mom responded.

So this past Thanksgiving weekend, I reluctantly returned home to Tucson, Arizona to begin cleaning out the two-decade-old treasure trove that I once swore would only be sold to pay for my kid's college fund.

I arrived in town like a cast member of *American Pickers*. It had been so long since I had explored my collection of stuff, I wasn't sure what was still in that closet. After all, it had been *nineteen years*. I wasn't sure if moths had eaten away at everything, or if I would discover some long lost prize that would pay off my student loans and credit card debt.

When I opened the door to the lost tomb of my childhood, I was immediately hit with a warm wave of nostalgia; I felt transported back to being that 13-year-old screaming at Ken Griffey, Jr. for an autograph in 1988. Everything was there. All the busted bats I had convinced players like Joe Carter and Cory Snyder to give me during Spring Training. The scores of batting practice foul balls I had gathered and had signed by onetime major league prospects like David Taylor and Craig Smajstrla. Tens of thousands of baseball cards. Other souvenirs included pine tar rags, batting gloves, and lineup cards from my days following the Tucson Toros and the Cleveland Indians. I had stored unopened Kraft macaroni and cheese boxes that had cut-out baseball cards of Angels' rookie Wally Joyner on the back panel, adjacent to a Michael Jordan Wheaties box. I even found a few Kathy Ireland *Sports Illustrated* Swimsuit Issues that had been dear companions to me on lonely junior high afternoons…

It was a beautiful assemblage of my long lost childhood. I couldn't quite figure out where to start.

From1981 until about 1990, I rearranged my bedroom in a tribute to the game of baseball. Don Mattingly was my boyhood hero, and box scores, batting averages, and ERA's practically ran my life for nine splendid and unforgettable years during my adolescence.

When other kids went to Golf-N-Stuff on the weekend to meet the cute 6th grade girls like Amy Foust and Erin Shelly, I went to Tucson's premiere baseball card shop, The Sports Page, with my collector-geek friends. My mother would often walk by my room and see me obsessing over Dave Winfield's career batting average or Rickey Henderson's stolen base record and casually mention that she had heard some of my other friends were going to a local water park with some classmates… I offered up a simple shrug of my shoulders and poured directly back into rearranging my baseball cards, occasionally choosing to alphabetize them so that I would always be able to pull them out at any given moment.

Girls were certainly around, but I was way too insecure to ever do anything about them. I left the girls at school to the skater kids dressed in Vision Street Wear with their designer Gator skateboards.

Me? I was Vice President of the baseball card club at my junior high and a hip-hop fan who used to write songs like "The Baseball Card Rap" to perform with some of my friends at a school talent show.

Basically, I was a fucking geek.

My parents seemed to never truly understand my obsession with "America's pastime". Perhaps it was because my own personal baseball career had come to an abrupt end when I broke my arm in fifth grade. My much-hyped Little

League comeback fell through and I hit a combined .216 over the next three seasons. I found my true baseball success in collecting memorabilia and autographs from big league ballplayers.

My mom could only stare in bewilderment as her oldest son spent all his allowance and Bar Mitzvah money on what she viewed as mere pieces of cardboard. In fact, the only time I remember talking to my mom about baseball cards was when I asked if I could fly to her childhood home in New Jersey to look in the attic for all those Mickey Mantle rookies she claimed her mom once threw away.

My travel wishes were never granted.

Back in the present, I started picking through my closet at a snail's pace. Initially, it was mind-blowing.

I was taken back to those hot summers spent in Revco drug stores scrambling for the newest cards, slipping Wade Boggs rookies into plastic album sleeves, and standing outside in the 92 degree Tucson heat trying to get minor league players like Craig Biggio to sign a baseball. Sorting through the cards was like revisiting old friends: Mattingly's clean-shaven face on his '84 Donruss rookie, Dwight Gooden's pre-cocaine gold tooth on his '85 Fleer card, even Ryne Sandberg's impossible youth on 1983 Topps rookie that I had traded for back in 1985. Every scrapbook, picture and signature recalled a memory of a childhood full of innocence and a passionate love for the game of baseball; I was suddenly 11-years-old again.

For the first hour, going through common cards and rediscovering lost names like Alvaro Espinoza and Steve Sax was both magical and cathartic. However, when I came across a poorly-forged Mark McGwire autographed baseball shoved deep inside my closet, I suddenly burst into tears.

The first friend I had ever had in my life was a kid named Nathan. Our parents had lived together when we were born, two months apart, in 1975. At age two, Nathan's family split Tucson and moved back east to Fairfield, Connecticut. My family stayed in Tucson. Still, by that time, a brotherly bond had already been formed and as the years moved on, Nathan and I grew closer through written correspondence, summer travel, and phone calls.

Around first grade, we discovered that we shared an intense passionate love for the New York Yankees, forced upon us by our fathers. We had also both inherited an extensive collection of baseball cards from older kids who had moved on to skateboards and girls, and we both began adding to them with fervor. As the years rolled on, our friendship grew alongside our collections.

In 1983, I went to my first Yankees game with Nathan and our dads; we were playing against George Brett and the Kansas City Royals, the day before the Pine Tar Game. Dave Winfield hit a home run, and Nathan and I split five hot dogs and 3,000 calories in stadium treats. A lifelong obsession had been kicked into high gear; I still remember Winfield's homer soaring into the bullpen and that first view of the infield as we walked up from the escalator. I get chills just thinking about it.

As the years rolled along, Nathan and I continued to share our baseball card collecting stories through the mail. However, it wasn't until 1986 or so, when I began obtaining hundreds of players' signatures at Spring Training, that Nathan began to get somewhat jealous of my collection. At the time, if you were a kid in Tucson you could walk up to Hi Corbett Field and practically stand in the on-deck circle as the teams warmed up to play each other. My buddies and I would skip school and get to the field to watch guys like Mark Grace and Rob Deer take batting practice before snagging their signatures. It was the end of an era, when ballplayers still made the league minimum of $62,500 and didn't face any threat of being harassed or jumped by some stupid drunk fan hanging around the dugout. Odly enough, these were also the last days of Dollar Beer Night.

As my autograph collection grew, more and more collectors from across the country began asking me to get them signed baseballs from the superstars of the day like Canseco and McGwire (way before the steroid era and Canseco's tell-all book *Juiced)*.Realizing that I had an inside advantage over any collector from say, Vermont, I recognized a little business opportunity.

So, I began charging a fee.

It was actually Nathan's idea to charge. I was so adept at getting autographs, I would charge five dollars to a guy in Nebraska for a Canseco ball and maybe a little bit more for a team ball. I went to at least 25 games that spring and got everything I could signed. From there, it was sold, stamped, and shipped. By the end of spring training, I had made roughly $375 and was buying any baseball card I wanted at The Sports Page. I had become an entrepreneur, making easy money.

And it was about to get easier.

That August, Nathan wrote me a letter and suggested a way to make even *more* money.

"Have you ever considered *forging* the autographs?"

I was on it like Tony Gwynn on a knee-high fastball. Within days, I had mastered every All-Star's signature. I spent hours perfecting Will Clark's swooping "W", Mark McGwire's curvaceous bubble "M", and Dwight Gooden's huge, elongated "D". I had handwriting intonations down pat; I was suddenly, a MASTER FORGER.

Nathan came to visit the following spring and proceeded to take back about fifty forged items to Connecticut. We had agreed that he would sell them and we'd split the profits. Within two weeks, after convincing his local baseball card shop that he had been collecting autographs in Arizona at Spring Training, he had pulled in *750 dollars*.

All on 100 percent forged material.

Back then, our operation was so easy to pull off because nobody would question 13-year-old kids who were selling really legitimate-looking autographs. In the years following, I have read about dozens of teenagers and adults getting arrested and caught in the forgery game. I guarantee that if you ever bought an autographed baseball or card in Fairfield, Connecticut or Tucson, Arizona during the late 1980's, Nathan and I had something to do with it…I'm sorry.

I am happy to say that we got out before there was any industry crackdown. Our little gig continued for a few years, until Nathan and I both stopped caring about baseball cards and retired from the forgery racket about $2,500 richer. Girls and music and pot had entered our lives and we suddenly realized that maybe those cool skater kids had the right idea all along.

Holding the poorly forged McGwire ball, I thought about Nathan. He had passed away fifteen years before at the age of 21, long before we ever got to reunite and laugh about our little criminal business venture.

As I sat on the floor of my childhood bedroom, I could see the nerves behind the shaky hand that had forged the ball back in 1987. It was a touching return to the last days of my innocence; long before I followed a girl named

Leslie around the country on the heels of a Grateful Dead tour hoping she would consider me as a boyfriend, before overdue bills and property taxes and a family of my own to feed…and long before Nathan's demons got the best of him.

And now, here was my mother demanding that I throw away everything in my closet. I decided to take a stand.

"Mom, I can't do this right now," I screamed from across the house.

"Oh shut up and get rid of that crap," she responded.

I wiped the tears from my eyes and approached her in the living room five minutes later. I sat down and relayed some of the stories and forgery adventures I had shared with Nathan all those years ago and told her I wasn't able to emotionally get through the memories stored in the closet just yet. Having recently lost her best friend to cancer, my mother sat me down and talked me through it.

She totally understood. She also informed me that it had been fifteen years since his death and that I needed to get over it. She had been forced to clean out her best friend's house in San Francisco just after she had passed away a year earlier. All I had to do was throw away some baseball cards and get back to my family in Los Angeles. It was as intense a moment as I have ever shared with my mother, and we have never felt closer.

After agreeing to keep a few items, but sell the majority of the cards to a baseball card shop, I managed to get through the rest of my closet somewhat easily. I found some special bits and pieces that, worthless or not, meant the world to me and tucked them away for my son.

My grandfather's Christy Mathewson card passed down from my uncle for my Bar Mitzvah.

A Craig Biggio Tucson Toros cap.

Even that 1984 Donruss Don Mattingly card.

The rest of my collection was bundled up into a box and headed to a baseball card shop. I decided I was going to sell it all to The Sports Page.

I dialed the number from memory, expecting to hear Mike or Orby answer the way they did back in 1988.

Instead, a woman answered. She did not work at The Sports Page.

She went on to inform me that the shop had closed roughly fifteen years earlier, and that she used to get people calling her looking for it all the time. Turns out, I was the first caller looking for The Sports Page in about nine years.

Wow. *Had it been that long?*

I eventually managed to find another store in Tucson willing to look at my collection. As I brought the nearly 120,000 cards into the shop, I looked around at the changing face of what was once my obsession. Gone were the display cases full of modern rookie cards. The new collector's items of choice were LeBron James or Kobe Bryant autographed game-worn jerseys, both of which came with a certificate of authenticity. I couldn't blame 'em.

I sat and talked to the two baseball card employees for roughly 45 minutes about the changing face of collecting, the effect eBay had on the hobby, and its future. After they scoured through my cards, they told me there wasn't really much they'd be interested in, and I told them I kind of figured that would be the case. They suggested Goodwill. I admired a Derek Jeter autographed baseball mitt in a glass case and a Josh Hamilton Texas Rangers signed bat before thanking my new friends for their time.

However, before I packed it all in and left for the parking lot, they informed me that if I had any autographed items of value I'd be willing to sell I should come back and they would take a look.

I surveyed the store and thought long and hard.

"Well, I *do* have a Mark McGwire autographed baseball…"

I looked towards the sky. Nathan would be so proud…

www.ingramcontent.com/pod-product-compliance
Lightning Source LLC
LaVergne TN
LVHW022317080426
835509LV00036B/2179
* 9 7 8 0 9 8 3 7 2 3 7 3 8 *